getting organized

IMPROVING FOCUS, ORGANIZATION AND PRODUCTIVITY

advanced-common-sense

Also by Chris Crouch

The Contented Achiever (with Don Hutson and George Lucas)
Simple Works (with Susan Drake)

People are Saying...

"There is richness and texture to *Getting Organized* that one wouldn't expect to find when thinking about organization. In addition to providing excellent, easy-to-implement ideas for increasing focus, organization and productivity, *Getting Organized* inspires people to live and work in a more conscious and meaningful way."

Barbara Browning
Order Within, Owner
Bayside, California

"If you want to reduce the stress and anxiety in your life caused by lack of focus, organization and productivity, then this is the book to read! It will help you achieve peace, harmony and balance in both your personal and professional life. This book is SIMPLY the best."

Debbie Hoover, Owner
Back on Track! Solutions
Forth Worth, Texas

"I've tried every 'time management' system out there, but I still felt that I was on top of everything but couldn't get to the bottom of anything. By using the ideas presented in *Getting Organized*, I can focus, prioritize and manage that paper tsunami that used to cover my desk!"

Kathleen Alessandro, President
Energized Solutions, LLC
Allen Park, Michigan

"Why follow the suggestions in this book? Because they WORK. Get unstuck by applying what you read here."

Kris Pond-Burtis, Ph.D.
Business and Professional Organizer and Trainer
Krisalis, Inc.
Waterloo, Iowa

"Proven, practical and easy to use: *Getting Organized* is for anyone who wants less chaos and stress, and who doesn't want to spend a lot of time implementing solutions. Chris Crouch cuts out the usual information overload and presents strategies that readers can understand easily and use immediately."

Lise Stahl Brown, President
artful Productivity
Concord, Massachusetts

"Getting Organized takes the overstress, overwork and overwhelm of today's business environment and makes things manageable. This simple and structured system creates order, priority and balance in just minutes a day."

Elizabeth Kachoris, Consultant and Trainer
Finely Focused
Chicago, Illinois area

"Getting Organized is engaging, accessible and grounded in the real world. It's my favorite training resource, because the storytelling format gives these great ideas "stickiness" in a way that never happens with a bunch of bullet points."

Kate S. Brown, Partner
Impact Organizing/Training & Consulting
Sarasota, Florida

"The ideas in *Getting Organized* are not only extremely effective, they are easy to understand and implement. This makes it more likely that people will continue to use them and continue to reap the many benefits of being organized."

J. Keith Sterne, CPA, CFP, CEBS
Germantown, Tennessee

"Want to be remarkable at work and have time for fun? Read *Getting Organized*. It's simple, effective and life changing. This book is a must!"

Anne Sedler
HFD Productivity Associates
Ridgewood, New Jersey

"Life doesn't have to be difficult. Chris Crouch shows us how to make life balanced, focused and ultimately easier."

Ann Michael Henry, President
Mise En Place
Rochester, New York

"Being more focused, organized and productive has never been easier to achieve, more compelling and genuinely fascinating than after reading *Getting Organized*."

Betsy Tookmanian, President
b. organized, inc.
West Chester, Pennsylvania

"When I read *Getting Organized*, I thought it was brilliant in its simplicity. I implemented many of the ideas the very next day. Finally, the organizational solution I had been looking for!"

Jan Keller
JTK Training
Golden, Colorado

"Chris teaches us that getting organized is about more than clearing up clutter. With profoundly simple ideas and a step-by-step method, Chris shows us how to create the habits and beliefs that help us get organized and stay organized. Applying his insights has allowed me to help many of my clients unlock their best professional selves."

Cristin Lind
Productivity and Organizing Consultant
Somerville, Massachusetts

"Who doesn't want prosperity, bliss and harmony?! Chris presents essential strategies to focus, prioritize and organize our life and work in order to pursue the projects, people and possibilities that are our passion. Read, act and realize your prosperity!"

Judy Siebert, Educator and Consultant
Back on Track! Solutions
Iowa City, Iowa

"Getting Organized is a wonderful tool that provides a foundation for being more productive. I encourage clients to use it as a reference book after the initial reading to help them change old unproductive habits into new productive habits."

Rena Hanks, Owner
Rena Hanks Consulting
Sparks, Nevada

"Chris provides simple ways to organize your life that anyone can follow and stick to. This book is definitely worth your time and money. Best book on the market for getting organized."

Janice Gentles-Jones, Productivity Consultant
Gentles Consulting
Westbury, New York

"Clarity and simplicity are at the heart of *Getting Organized.* Chris definitely makes the difficult easy to tackle with his realistic solutions to facilitate decluttering and organizing."

Eileen Stevie, President
Stevie Organizing Services
Cary, North Carolina

"Absorbing Chris Crouch's world-class ideas into my consulting practice has been a gift beyond measure - to me and to my clients. Chris' concepts are true treasures."

Kate Harper, President
Harper Systems
Berkeley, California

"Getting Organized provides ideas you will not only use for the rest of your life, but you will want to share them with everyone you come in contact with who wants to stay focused, organized and productive."

Wendy Ellin, President
Momentum
Atlanta, Georgia

"*Getting Organized* goes beyond just getting people organized, it changes people's lives. We continue to seek tools that will help our associates become more efficient, productive and lead a balanced life. With *Getting Organized* and the *GO System*, they can do all three. We have currently trained 300+ associates and we don't see ourselves stopping. We continue to add eager participants to our waiting list. The word is spreading fast on how effective the *GO System* is and we continue to receive comments like '*The GO System works. Already others, seeing my clean desk have asked about the 'secret'. Thanks for the great course; it can truly change your world.*' "

Jill Pheffer, Personal and Professional Development Specialist
Baird University
Robert W. Baird & Co.
Milwaukee, Wisconsin
FORTUNE "100 Best Companies to Work For"
2004, 2005, 2006 and 2007

"I work with clients who are overwhelmed with piles of papers, lists of daily tasks and a mosaic of sticky notes on their computer screens. After implementing the *GO System* for a client, he greeted me with, 'You have changed my life!' You'll find the same results from reading *Getting Organized*."

Julie Mahan, President
Simply Organizing, Inc.
Indianapolis, Indiana

"It is so rewarding to see my clients so excited after reading *Getting Organized*. They love the ideas that allow them to stay on top of their daily workload and they feel good about having the systems and processes to deal with what they face each day. Thanks Chris for such a wonderful book!"

Cathy Sexton
CSBS LLC - Creating Simple Business Solutions
Fenton, Missouri

"This is, by far, the best book I recommend on getting organized. I try to encourage my clients to keep things simple, and *Getting Organized* explains things in a way that everyone can comprehend and implement."

Dawn Gimm, Professional Organizer/Productivity Consultant
QC Organizing Solutions, LLC
Bettendorf, Iowa

"Simply put...*Getting Organized* provides solutions to problems that are stressing people out! I've been in the organizing business for almost 10 years, and it feels great to finally have the tools in a simple format that people understand."

Sue DeRoos
Organize U
Macomb, Illinois

"As I continue to apply the ideas presented in *Getting Organized*, my day is calmer and I am able to stay more focused. Also, I get a great sense of satisfaction helping others experience the same."

Jan Tyner, Owner
TNT Training
Tulsa, Oklahoma area

"Chris Crouch has an amazing ability to boil down what he knows into nuggets of gold that can be shared with others in a way that is very easy to grasp. This book is a must-read for those seeking to live a more productive and balanced life."

Kathy Paauw
Productivity Consultant/Coach
Redmond, Washington

"I recommend *Getting Organized* in group training sessions and when consulting with individuals and suggest taking a 'buffet approach' when reading it. Pick the ideas that resonate with you and pass on any that don't apply. However, most people find that most - if not all - of the ideas DO apply and work GREAT!"

Christine Kominiak, Owner
Productive Sense Training and Consulting
Albuquerque, New Mexico

"As a professional productivity consultant and trainer, I was surprised how much my own productivity increased utilizing the techniques in *Getting Organized*. I easily capture my ideas and tasks, transfer them into a system that really works - and the ease of prioritization is the icing on the cake."

Kristin Maria Hébert
GO Productivity
Miami, Florida

"*Getting Organized* is the first organizing book that I have read cover to cover after being in the organizing profession for seven years. It is easy to read, easy to comprehend, and full of practical ideas that I know work!"

Carla Miller, Productivity Consultant
This Way Up
Dallas, Texas

getting organized

IMPROVING FOCUS, ORGANIZATION AND PRODUCTIVITY

Chris Crouch

Dawson

PUBLISHING

This publication is designed to provide reliable information regarding the subject matter covered. It is sold with the understanding that the author and publisher are not engaged in rendering psychological, legal, financial, or other professional advice. If expert assistance is required, the services of a professional should be sought.

Copyright © 2005, 2006, 2007 by Chris Crouch

Published by Dawson Publishing
3410 S. Tournament Drive
Memphis, TN 38125

The *GO System*® and *Advanced Common Sense*® are registered trademarks of DME Training and Consulting.

Cover design: Venue Advertising

Printed in the United States

10 9 8 7 6 5 4 3

Publisher's Cataloging-in-Publication
(Provided by Quality Books, Inc.)

Crouch, Chris.
    Getting organized : learning how to focus, organize, and prioritize / Chris Crouch.
    p. cm.
    LCCN 2004109366
    ISBN-10: 0-9758-6809-8
    ISBN-13: 978-0-9758-6809-6

    1. Paperwork (Office practice)--Management--Handbooks, manuals, etc. I. Title.

HF5547.15.C76 2005   651.5
                                  QBI04-200294

Special discounts are available on quantity purchases by corporations, associations and others. For details, please call Dawson Publishing at 901-748-2142 or write to the address above.

Dedication

This book is dedicated to my wonderful children David, Diana and Kathryn, and my granddaughter Caitlin. They continue to learn things at a much earlier age than I finally learned them. I also dedicate this book to my parents who won't believe their son, who formerly lived in such a messy room, has written a book on getting organized.

Contents

The Big Picture

Although learning the processes and techniques that make up what I refer to as the *GO System* training course will serve you well in many areas of your life, the primary goal of the course is:

Improving focus, organization and productivity in the workplace

That's the "Big Picture" of what this book is also about - becoming more focused, organized and productive... and improving your work performance. Large companies frequently spend millions of dollars on training programs to accomplish these end results. That makes perfect sense. Well-trained, competent people get superior results. That, of course, is a very good thing.

What does not make any sense (that seems to go on every day in many large, medium and small organizations) is spending money on training people to perform highly specialized skills and tasks *before they have mastered the day-to-day processes related to getting and staying focused, organized and productive.* This is a foundational concept that applies to successfully running any organization. In other words, you should consider the proper sequence of training events before you invest your training dollars. Plain English translation: *Don't keep spending money on the complex stuff until you have taken care of the basics. Don't try to build a culture of superior performers on a shaky foundation of unfocused, unorganized, unproductive people. Don't waste training dollars!*

For example, what good does it do to commit time, money and energy to a sophisticated sales training course for your sales representatives if they:

- Operate in an extremely cluttered environment and can't even maintain reasonable order in their workspace?

- Can't effectively and efficiently process and follow up on their incoming paper, e-mails, voice mails, etc?

- Can't seem to establish, determine, or stick to their priorities?

- Haven't learned to use their time in a rational manner?

- Can't seem to stay focused on…or follow up and get closure on…simple tasks and projects?

- Can't handle many of the basic skills critical to their success?

Should you buy these people more sophisticated computers, cell phones, personal digital assistants, and other gadgets if they haven't even learned to handle the basics? By the way, it's not totally their fault that they haven't mastered some of these basics. They don't teach much of this stuff in schools. Once again, if you consider the "Big Picture", it doesn't seem to make much sense to invest more in people who haven't mastered the basics. By contrast, when you get everyone in your organization focused on the basics, good things quickly start happening.

This book is full of ideas and suggestions that:

- Are simple to understand

- Are easy to implement

- Are focused on mastering the basics of becoming more focused, organized and productive

If you are seriously ready to get organized, here's another version of the "Big Picture" related to this book:

This is the horse that goes before the cart!

Enjoy the book. Try the ideas you like...ignore the ones you don't.

I wish you much success!

Chris

Acknowledgements

As you read *Getting Organized*, you will quickly discover that many of the ideas in the book, perhaps most, are not new ideas. When I began to seriously study this topic, I read books, listened to tapes, viewed videos, went to courses on getting organized and talked with professional trainers in the organizing business. My goal was to sift through the resources and discover ideas that were effective, low cost, low tech and easy to try. I am grateful for all the people who shared their ideas with me through their books, tapes, videos and courses. I offer special thanks to Don Hutson, Maynard Rolston, Barbara Hemphill and our excellent group of Certified *GO System* Trainers who continue to offer support and ideas that have helped us maintain a rewarding training and consulting business.

I spend a lot of my time studying and thinking. But studying and thinking alone will not create anything tangible. Someone must follow through and make tangible things happen. Robin Thomas and I have a very unique partnership. I think of my side of our business as the "idea farm" and she runs the "product factory" side. I develop and nurture ideas and she turns them into books, course material and other tangible products. I am typically thought of as the creative one of the partnership, but Robin actually creates everything tangible that is offered by our company. She and her friend Tamra FitzGerald (and Tamra's wonderful support group including Denise Carter who edited this book, Louise Scopelitis who designed the cover, Teca Sullivan who helps manage the details, and others) at Venue Advertising do an incredible job of designing and producing materials to help me convert my ideas into training resources. Without them, there would be no tangible evidence of my work.

Thanks to all the people who bought copies of my previous books, and thanks to Dawson...wherever you are.

getting organized

IMPROVING FOCUS, ORGANIZATION AND PRODUCTIVITY

Introduction

Welcome to *Getting Organized*, a collection of simple ideas to help you become more focused, organized and productive. In order to help you convert these ideas into action in your day-to-day life, each idea is presented in a three-part format. I explain the idea (What?), explain why the idea is important or how the idea may affect you (So What?), and suggest how you can use the idea (Now What?). Let's begin by using this format to explain the reason for this approach.

What?

Years ago, I attended a seminar conducted by Gary O'Malley of O'Malley Associates. He gave us a handout full of great ideas, including information on how to process the ideas presented in the course. The handout stated you should think about the following each time you encounter a new idea:

Think about...	In other words...	The related process...
What?	What idea is conveyed?	Receiving information
So What?	How does this affect me?	Reflection
Now What?	What will I do about it?	Application

So What?

It seems to make a lot of sense to use this process to provide structure for a book on getting organized. If you are reading a book on how to get organized, I suspect you want to get to the point. You are probably looking for simple ideas presented in a straightforward and easy-to-digest manner. You have no need for confusion, complexity or unnecessary information. I don't think I can come up with a better book-writing process – for this type of book – than the system outlined in Gary's handout...so I'll use his three-step process.

Now What?

Now you know what to expect if you choose to read this book. The chapters are short and always include three sections. The first section gives you information on the idea. The second section tells you more about the idea and how it might affect you. The third section suggests what you can do with the idea. As a reader, this makes your part simple...take a quick look at the idea, try the ideas you like, discard the ones you don't.

The writer Sydney Smith said:

"The writer does the most who gives the reader the most knowledge and takes from him the least time."

I'm going to try my best to live up to Sydney's advice in this book. Thank you for choosing to share some time with me as you read *Getting Organized*. I am honored to share these thoughts with you and hope these ideas help you accomplish your personal goals and dreams...whatever they may be!

1
Why Can't I Get Organized?

What?

Many people desperately want to get more organized but can't seem to stick with their organizing plan. That's because at least six major issues generate chaos and disorder in most people's lives. All six issues must be addressed in order to get organized and stay organized.

So What?

Imagine you are planning to go on a trip in your car. You are excited, motivated and ready to go! As you approach your car, you notice it has a flat tire. Then you realize the car is out of gas, the battery is dead, the transmission is broken, the steering wheel is locked up and the starter will not work. How far do you think you are going to get in this car on this day? You are going nowhere until you fix not just one, but six things that are wrong with the car. Any one of these issues will prevent you from making any forward progress in this vehicle. This car doesn't just need a quick fix…it needs a major overhaul. Like the broken car, there are six issues that prevent you from making forward progress on your plan to get organized:

1. Efficiently handling incoming items (paper, e-mails, voice mails, verbal requests, and things you think of that you want to do)

2. Prioritizing your workload (making sure you are working on the most important item)

3. Time management (rational vs. irrational use of your time)

4. Project management (taking an idea from inception to closure)

5. Personality issues (understanding how personality attributes impact tasks to be completed)

6. Psychological issues (dealing with self-defeating and dysfunctional behavior)

For example, you may have the most efficient and effective paper-handling process known to mankind, but it does you no good if your tendency to procrastinate has reached the dysfunctional behavior level. Like the car with six problems, you will get nowhere with your organizing plan until you address all six of these issues. You may be fortunate. Maybe you do not have significant problems with all six of the above issues. But any one of these issues alone can create plenty of chaos in your life.

Now What?

All six of the above issues are addressed in this book. If you feel you need more help in a particular area, additional resources are listed in the back of the book.

In the broken car example, some of you would have little or no interest in fixing the car. You would just buy a new one and head out on your trip. However, the car probably ended up in such bad shape due to neglect. Most of the problems could have been avoided with a little preventive maintenance on the front end. If you buy a new car and do not change your preventive maintenance habits, the problems will soon reappear in the new car. Then you are back where you started...with the added burden of a new car payment.

Getting organized works the same way. There are many simple things you can do on the front end to prevent disorganization. Subtract your age from 85. That's how long most of you have left to live. That's how long you have left to enjoy an organized life if you go ahead and learn how to get organized now. Go ahead and do a major overhaul on your organizing plan. Fix it right this time and enjoy the benefits for years to come. Look for ideas in this book to help you prevent disorganization before it creeps into your life and destroys your productivity and happiness.

Remember, there are six issues that prevent you from making forward progress on your plan to get organized.

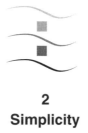

2
Simplicity

What?

Two things keep many people from trying something new:

1. They think it's too hard to try.

2. They think it's too simple to work.

Many of the ideas in this book may, in fact, appear too simple to work. *Don't let some of my Forrest Gump-like ideas keep you from giving them a try.*

So What?

As the story goes, when NASA first started sending astronauts into space, they quickly discovered that garden-variety ballpoint pens would not work in zero gravity. They snapped into action, spent tons of money and developed a zero-gravity pen...problem solved! Their Russian counterparts had the same problem, but did not have the vast resources to throw at the problem, so they gave their cosmonauts pencils. This simple solution worked at a significantly lower cost! In reality, this is only a myth. However, the idea of keeping things simple makes a lot of sense.

Now What?

Try some of the ideas in this book. Don't just read about them...try them! Remember, you can't lose weight by simply reading a diet book. You can't learn to cook by simply reading a cookbook. You can't get organized by simply reading a book on getting organized. You accomplish things by putting theory into action...by trying the ideas presented in the books.

"It is very hard to be simple enough to be good."

— Ralph Waldo Emerson

3
Physical Activity Always Follows Mental Activity

What?

Don't just think fast...think first!

"All that man achieves and all that he fails to achieve is the direct result of his own thoughts."

So What?

This quote is from a great book titled *As a Man Thinketh* by James Allen. It is one of the most powerful books you can read and it illustrates the point of this chapter...you cannot stay organized until you change the thought patterns that drive your daily activities. *The mental side of getting organized is significantly more important than anything else you can do.* If you want to get organized and stay organized, get your mind right and the rest will easily follow.

Is your office cluttered? Are you always in a rush and complaining that you don't have enough time to get it all done? What image do you suppose this is projecting to others around you? What do they think of your chaotic manner of operating? How would you like to have an operation performed by a surgeon or fly with an airline pilot who operated in this manner?

Many people continually advertise (and often verbalize and brag about) how busy and stressed-out they are. They try to gain sympathy by telling everyone about their heroic efforts to overcome their overwhelming circumstances. They are, of course, also interested in getting promoted, gaining more responsibility and making more money. Their managers typically look at them and wonder, "How can I give them any more responsibility?" Their customers wonder, "How can they handle my account? They can't handle what they have now. They are already in over their heads!"

Now What?

Over the next few days, try to increase your level of awareness about how many things you are doing automatically...without really thinking. This can be good news or bad news. Look for those times when it is bad news. If you feel the pressure starting to build up, your natural response is often to speed up and chase after things, rather than slowing down and thinking about what you are doing. For the next few days, when you feel that you are under a lot of pressure, slow down and think about what you are doing and determine the most productive use of your time. Under stress, many people default to counterproductive or low-value actions (overeating, overdrinking, reading worthless e-mails, going to worthless meetings, cleaning out their middle desk drawer, etc.). Learn to default to a productive activity instead...think!

As Einstein said, "Problems can't be solved at the same level of consciousness that created them." Think about it!

4
Get Your Habits Right and Defeat the Beast

What?

Within you resides a beast that has the potential to devour your energy, focus and productivity. For lack of a better term, let's call it the Beast of Disorganization. The Beast feeds on bad habits! The Beast absolutely loves bad habits! It cannot survive without them. The Beast especially loves the fact that disorganized people don't think of simply changing their habits, but seem to look everywhere else for solutions to their problems. *If you are not currently organized, there is a good chance you will never get organized or stay organized until you change some of your counterproductive, chaos-generating habits.*

So What?

It's fairly simple. You have some habits that help you live an organized life and some that lead to chaos and disorganization. *Identify and change the habits that are creating the disorganized part of your life if you want to get organized. Set up processes and systems to help support and encourage your good habits.* Don't make getting organized any more complicated than that.

Now What?

A good first step is assigning the responsibility for any disorganization you are experiencing in your life where it belongs...to your counterproductive habits. Very few people seem to seriously address their habits when they decide to get organized. People usually try to solve the problem by buying planners, calendars, personal digital assistants, software and all kinds of gadgets and devices that promise to quickly solve the problem...and then wonder why they don't work. They may work for a short period of time, but when the newness wears off, the old habits are just sitting there waiting to nurture the Beast.

Some people do try to change the habits that are causing their problems, but they don't stick with the program long enough. It usually takes 21 to 30 days to starve the Beast.

If you want to stay highly organized, think in terms of *habit-based solutions* (as opposed to gadget-based solutions). There are a lot of habits suggested in this book. This book also offers processes and systems to help you form and maintain these productive habits. When you maintain these habits, you will significantly increase the chances that you will get organized and stay organized.

**Habits are either the best of servants
or the worst of masters.**

5
The Monkey Trap

What?

When you read the following story about how hunters trap monkeys, you may think…monkeys are incredibly stupid! However, read on before you judge monkeys too harshly. There are several versions of the monkey trap story, but they all have one thing in common. The monkey gets his hand in a tight place, such as a jar, vase or coconut and can't seem to figure out how to get it out. He gets trapped!

As one story goes, the monkey hunters cut a small hole or slit in a coconut and fill it with rice. Then they tie the coconut to a tree or attach it to a stake in the ground. The hole in the coconut is big enough for the monkey to get his hand in, but not big enough to get his hand out if it is filled with rice. As the hunters approach, the monkey desperately tries to get his fist out of the coconut, but can't seem to understand that gaining his freedom is simply a matter of letting go of the rice.

So What?

The most important element of the monkey trap is the monkey (or it could be you or me if we are acting like a trapped monkey). The trap will not work without his full cooperation. Keep this in mind!

Now What?

Failure to let go of outdated and unproductive ways of doing things serve as monkey traps for all of us. For example, there is a file maintenance product on the market called Taming the Paper Tiger® that is extremely impressive. It is a piece of software that works like an Internet search engine. Imagine having all your reference files set up with a Google-like search engine. The product advertises that you can find anything in your files in five seconds or less. I have been using it for several years and *it has never let me down*. The average person spends 30 minutes to two hours a day looking for things in their office. Therefore, this product can save you a tremendous amount of time every day! Why doesn't everyone use it? It is totally counterintuitive for most people. For one thing, you file items numerically instead of alphabetically. Once you use it for just a short while, it makes perfect sense. But most people are caught in the monkey trap. They can't let go of their old way of filing things. So they give up the opportunity to easily free up huge blocks of time and get rid of huge amounts of frustration.

How many people do you know who are caught in monkey traps? They can't let go of the old ways of doing things. How many corporate perks are keeping people in jobs they hate? How many large mortgages or car payments are serving as monkey traps for people? Monkey traps are everywhere!

Look for old ways of doing things that are keeping you from getting organized. Let them go! It's the equivalent of letting go of the handful of rice and pulling your hand out of the coconut. Stop thinking like a monkey!

6
A Few Thoughts on Gadget-based Solutions

What?

Buying an electronic gadget, such as a personal digital assistant (PDA), and thinking you are going to be organized the next day is like buying a piano and thinking you are going to be able to play the piano the next day. When a disorganized person buys a PDA, the most likely outcome is frustration. Their days are already packed with enough things to do, and now they have another complex device to learn how to use and maintain.

Here's a general rule...*if you are not organized before you get a PDA or any other physical tool to help you get organized, you will not suddenly become organized after you get the tool.*

So What?

The true test of the value of an electronic gadget or piece of software is...is it easier to use than a pencil? PDAs are great for storing massive amounts of data when you are on the move. If I am out of town and I need my daughter's Social Security number, a friend's phone number or the address of a friend in the city I am visiting, my PDA is very handy. However, the core of every good organizing system is a calendar. I personally find it easier to keep up with my daily appointments with a simple, paper-based calendar and a pencil.

Once again, the process of getting organized *begins* with converting good decisions into good habits. It has been my observation that many people who struggle with staying organized ignore this "obvious" issue. They continue looking for the "silver bullet" in the form of a physical tool or gadget that will solve their problems, and ignore the fact that they must eventually change their thinking patterns and habits if they want to have any hope of getting organized.

Now What?

Identify the organizing habits you must develop before you select the other tools you will use to keep your life on track. If you have already spent a lot of money on various gadgets that failed to keep their promises, put them aside until you develop good organizing habits. Maybe they will work for you later, maybe they won't. Keep an open mind for now and don't allow them to become your monkey traps.

**Never assume the most recent invention
is the best invention (or solution).**

7
Right Now...!

What?

Years ago, I read a story about a woman who lived in La Jolla, Calif. She was an extremely high achiever and, on this particular day, she decided to walk her dog in a beautiful local park along the oceanfront. As she walked along, she thought of all the things on her to-do list. Several project deadlines were rapidly approaching, she had an upcoming event that required her to make the long journey to New York, she had family obligations to tend to, and the list went on and on. Her mind raced from thought to thought, trying to sort out her priorities. Suddenly she thought, *"Right now I am walking my dog in a beautiful park and that is what I should be focused on!"*

Fast-forward about two weeks. I am in my car headed for work. At this point in my life, I had a chronic car-buying virus. I loved nice automobiles! On this particular day, I decided to drive my nicest car-toy to work. As I headed down the interstate, my mind raced with all the things I had to do that day. I had meetings to attend, presentations to outline and prepare, slide shows to create...the list went on and on. Suddenly I thought, *"This is what that woman in La Jolla was doing...and now I'm doing it...I do it all the time!"* Then I thought, *"Right now I am driving one of the finest automobiles in the world and I am paying no attention to it!"* I pulled off at the next exit, let the top down on the car, chilled out and took the back roads to my office. The rest of my commute was delightful.

So What?

I decided to conduct a personal experiment. I knew you could install software programs to get computers to carry out specific assignments. Why not install some software in my brain to get it to do what I wanted it to do? I decided that anytime during the day I felt myself start to mentally wander or drift, I would think of the words *right now*…followed by whatever I was doing at the moment. For example, I thought, "Right now…I am talking with a customer, or right now…I am working on a speech, or right now…I am eating my lunch." It worked! *Repetition is one of the keys to success.* After a few weeks of doing this, it became a habit. It helped me learn to keep my physical and mental worlds in harmony. It was a huge turning point in my journey from being a disorganized person to a focused, organized person.

Now What?

One definition of focus is doing something and thinking about what you are doing at the same time. I know it sounds too simple, but give it a try. For the next few days, think about the two words "right now" as you go through your day and perform your duties. Use it to help concentrate and focus on important projects, pay closer attention to people you encounter, and enjoy life in general.

**Right now…think about this idea
and how you can use it!**

8
"To Do or Not To Do?"...That is the Question

What?

William Shakespeare was right. "Being" is more important than "doing." After all, we are human beings, not human doings. As a practical matter, right after you decide to "be or not to be" each morning, it's a good idea to ask yourself what you are *going to do* for the rest of the day. But don't stop there. Also ask what you are *not going to do*.

So What?

How you get started on an event or task often sets the tone for how the middle and end of the event or task will progress. When you get off to a good start, the rest often goes smoother. When you get off to a bad start, the rest often stays bad. This works in golf, relationships, careers and your life in general. Your life is made up of events called days, which make up weeks, which make up years, and so forth and so on. For the most part, life erases the board each day and allows you to get off to a fresh start. That is, unless you *choose* to continue the previous day's drama. Therefore, one of the most sensible things you can do if you want to have a good day...and a good life...is to simply get off to a good start. Rather than mindlessly plunging into tomorrow, living a "perpetual-sameness" life, why not make two good decisions that will help you get off to a good start? Why not purposely and consciously decide first thing in the morning what you are going to do and what you are not going to do?

Now What?

Don't make this hard. Simply think of the most important thing you need to do tomorrow and do it first thing in the morning. Don't allow anything, or any person, or any e-mail, or any phone call to distract you from whatever you feel is most important to you (not what is important to someone else). If you do not know what is most important to you, figuring that out is the exact thing you should be doing first thing in the morning. If you do not get in the habit of doing this, you will be doomed to living a channel-surfing life with someone else at the controls. Some of you will desperately want to make this idea more complicated than it is...don't go there!

Another candidate for the "most important thing you need to do tomorrow" category is... making a list of the things you are going to immediately stop doing. Learn a lesson from John Gagliardi, the legendary coach for Saint John's University football team. John Gagliardi is the winningest coach in football history. In the history of college football, there have been approximately 25,000 coaches. Of those, only 10 have won more than 300 games. John Gagliardi's teams have won over 400 games. John Gagliardi is the master of focusing on one thing at a time – the most important thing. He once said, "It's pretty hard to be undefeated unless you win the first game." He also is a master at eliminating things that do not matter. Among other items, he has eliminated the following in his coaching program: staff meetings, player meetings, playbooks, spring practices, tackling in practice and precision warm-up drills. He has become the winningest coach in football history by working on the most important thing and eliminating things that do not matter. Why don't you try doing the same?

What are you going to do first thing tomorrow?
What are you not going to do?

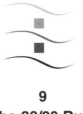

9
The 80/20 Rule

What?

Most people have heard of the 80/20 rule. Eighty percent of your results come from 20 percent of your efforts. That's another way of saying 80 percent of the things you do every day don't really matter. A lot of extremely smart people have scientifically and mathematically proven it's a pretty accurate assessment of reality.

So What?

Although this rule sounds simple, it is one of the most *powerful and overlooked* time-savers and productivity enhancers available. It is often overlooked because it is very counterintuitive. As humans, we are hardwired to believe our results are equal to our efforts. For example, 50 percent of our results come from 50 percent of our efforts and 60 percent of our results come from 60 percent of our efforts, and so on and so forth.

Even when people intellectually understand the 80/20 rule, they often fail to *translate it into changes* in the way they behave on a daily basis. It is easy to recognize when someone else is wasting time and doing things that do not matter; it is not so easy to see this in ourselves. People continue to complain about not having

enough time to get everything done and at the same time totally ignore the 80/20 rule.

Now What?

Here's an idea to try. If you work a typical eight-hour day…and
if you get 80 percent of your results from 20 percent of your
efforts…why not get real focused for 96 minutes each day (20
percent of eight hours)? Get a timer and set it for 96 minutes.
Focus, without interruptions, on your No. 1 priority for the day.
Try this as early in the day as possible, rather than getting
bogged down with e-mails, voice mails and other things that are
prime candidates for the 80 percent that doesn't matter. Many of
my clients and friends have tried this idea and told me it works
amazingly well. Try it for one week and see how well it works
for you.

> **Start your day with 96 minutes of concentrated
> work on your highest priority. Most days, these
> 96 minutes will be more than enough to call it
> a highly productive and successful day.**

10
The Best Reason to Get Organized

What?

You are more likely to get things done in your life if you have good reasons for doing them. Your reason for doing something should make you *feel good*. As it turns out, the fact that it makes you feel good *is* one of the best reasons to get organized.

So What?

Many people have forgotten how good it feels to be organized (or never knew in the first place). The closest they ever get to this wonderful feeling is the day before they go on vacation. That's the time when they finally buckle down and get their "act" together. Who likes to go on vacation with a lot of unfinished things hanging over their head? The day before vacation is when they finally get focused, get all the important things done, or at least under control, and end the day feeling great (remember I said most people, not all people)! Wouldn't it be nice to feel this way most days?

Now What?

When you start to feel overwhelmed and things seem to be getting out of control, imagine you are going on vacation the next day. Get focused on the important issues...the 20 percent that matters. Forget the unimportant...the 80 percent that does not matter. Look forward to the feeling you will have at the end of the day. Don't forget to enjoy the feeling you have *during the day*, when you know you are focused on important things, instead of getting caught in the busywork trap.

"There is no shortage of time. In fact, we are positively awash with it. We only make good use of 20 percent of our time."

— Richard Koch, *The 80/20 Principle*

11
Having a Definite Purpose

What?

The real, but rarely talked about, reason many people are unorganized is because they have an unorganized mind. It's no mystery to understand why this is a huge problem these days. Most people are being bombarded with sensory input and are completely overloaded. It's like the frog in the pot of hot water story. Little by little the heat is turned up until the frog gets boiled without knowing it.

So What?

Welcome to the frog-in-the-hot-pot-world! I don't have to tell you how the heat is being turned up on you. You can figure that out on your own. The bottom line is that we all have more sensory input and choices today than ever before. And more sensory input and choices lead to the following:

- Chaos
- Indecision
- Procrastination
- Mental Paralysis

It doesn't have to be this way! There is a solution…an antidote for an overloaded mind. It is called *having a definite purpose.*

Now What?

If you are struggling with procrastination, indecision or other issues related to an overloaded mind, the next best step for you is to *keep your mind busy with a definite purpose*. Slow down or stop the mental chaos by keeping your mind and body totally occupied with activities that directly relate to your life purpose for a reasonable amount of time each day. If you are not sure what you want to do with your life, start out by figuring out what you are going to do with today, the morning, or the next hour.

We all have a definite purpose, a calling. There is a reason we are on this planet at this time. You may think at this point I am getting a bit philosophical...and I am! But since this book is probably not going to end up in the philosophy section of the bookstores, let's get more practical.

If you know your definite purpose, start dropping out for at least an hour a day and focus on things that directly relate to it, whatever it is for you. Expand your amount of "drop out" time, when you feel ready, until you achieve a comfortable daily balance of "definite purpose" activities and other stuff. For example, I am a writer and a teacher. That's what I love to do. Anything that directly relates to writing and teaching makes me feel good about myself. It makes me feel as if I am absolutely on the right path in life. My life feels more focused and productive, and less chaotic. I've known this for years, but it took me a long time to back up this knowledge with action. Too often, I worked on "other stuff" first, so I could enjoy writing and teaching later. Recently, I made a new life decision. For the first half of every day, I write or teach. Everything else has to wait until after 10:36 a.m. Phone calls wait, e-mails wait, checking the stock market waits. Do I occasionally make exceptions? Sure, but they are extremely rare! I no longer allow a pattern of less important exceptions distract me from my definite life purpose. Don't allow the chaos of your daily life to get in the way of your life purpose. Decide today to "drop out" for an hour, two hours, or for whatever amount of time you need to focus on what's important to you.

If you don't know your definite purpose, spend one hour a day reading *Think and Grow Rich* by Napoleon Hill. It's not just another self-help book. It is a book that can help you discover your definite purpose and back it up with specific plans.

"The most practical of all methods for controlling the mind is the habit of keeping it busy with a definite purpose, backed by a definite plan."

— Napoleon Hill

12
Workaholic Behavior

What?

Workaholism is a common type of *dysfunctional behavior*. It is a destructive behavior pattern that is *not normal*. Simply working hard from time to time is not what I am talking about here. We all have to do that occasionally. It becomes dysfunctional when the duration and intensity of the behavior get out of control and begin affecting your life in a negative manner. Workaholics must fix this problem first if they want to get organized.

So What?

Many people actually brag about being workaholics. They love to tell you about how many hours they "put in" and how they haven't had a day off in months or years. Most workaholics do not realize they are, in effect, telling you they are dysfunctional and behaving in an irrational manner. There are only 24 hours in your day, only 24 hours in my day, only 24 hours in everybody's day.

- George Washington only had 24 hours each day to figure out how to build a new nation and follow up on his ideas.

- Dwight D. Eisenhower only had 24 hours each day to figure out how to win World War II and follow up on his ideas.

- Albert Einstein only had 24 hours each day to solve some of the greatest mysteries of the universe (including the true meaning of time).

These guys actually had some good reasons for occasionally being overloaded. The fact is, most of us are not building new nations, fighting global wars or solving the problems of the universe. We can probably get our work done without significantly over scheduling our workdays or turning into workaholics.

Now What?

Be honest with yourself (this may not be easy or feel good at first). Think about why you have *chosen* to be a workaholic. Here are some possible reasons according to psychologists who study this type of behavior:

- Workaholics have trouble relaxing or doing nothing. Some workaholics have a profound sense of insecurity and think that others appreciate them only for what they do instead of who they are.

- Workaholics have anxieties about not living up to expectations, not being good enough, or other people finding out they are not as good as everyone thinks they are. According to psychoanalyst Manfred Kets de Vries, these people put "all the eggs of self-esteem in the basket of work."

- Workaholics won't delegate because they think nobody else can do the work as well as they can. This attitude, of course, assures they will never escape from the workaholic cycle.

There are many other reasons for workaholism, but the more important issue is what to do about it. One of the best steps to conquer workaholism is to *take time out for reflection*. Figuring out why you are driving yourself so hard will help you figure out how to stop doing it. Use some of your restless energy to research the topic and figure out how to create a better, non-dysfunctional life for yourself. Stop thinking being a workaholic is normal behavior.

"There is more to life than to increase its speed."

— Mahatma Gandhi

13
Multitasking

What?

Occasionally, what we think of as multitasking is normal. It's still not a good idea, but we all have to do it from time to time. When multitasking becomes a way of life for you – the way you operate most of the time – it becomes dysfunctional behavior.

So What?

In February 2003, Sue Shellenbarger wrote an article for the *Wall Street Journal* about multitasking. The headline of her article was:

Multitasking Makes You Stupid:
Studies Show Pitfalls of Doing Too Much at Once

Here are a few highlights of the article:

- People who multitask are less efficient than those who focus on one project at a time.

- Managing two mental tasks at once reduces the brainpower available for either task.

- Trying to do two or three things at once, or in quick succession, can take longer than doing them one at a time.

Of course, there are many studies and research projects to back up the above claims. However, you don't need researchers to tell you the pitfalls of excessive multitasking. You probably know multitasking creates stress, short-term memory loss, and that it negatively impacts concentration and attentiveness.

Actually, some neuroscientists now believe there is no such thing as multitasking. What we think of as multitasking seems to involve rapidly flipping our attention between or among tasks. Switching your attention back and forth seriously undermines productivity.

Now What?

Slow down and focus on one thing at a time. Find the children's book about the tortoise and the hare and read it. Make a decision to stop being harebrained. Chapter 7 of this book discusses a technique called "right now." Reread that chapter and give it a try. Learn or rediscover the joys and rewards of doing one thing at a time.

Stay in the moment. Totally focus on what you are doing and get closure on it ... then move on to the next thing.

14
Clutter is Contagious

What?

There is a fascinating story about the "Broken Windows Theory" in a *New Yorker* magazine article by Malcolm Gladwell (see gladwell.com, June 3, 1996, article titled *The Tipping Point*). Stanford University psychologist Philip Zimbardo parked a car on a street in Palo Alto, Calif., where it sat untouched for a week. After a week, as a part of the experiment, Zimbardo smashed one of the car's windows with a sledgehammer. Within a few hours the car was stripped by vandals. Later, Gladwell wrote a book on the topic, also titled *The Tipping Point*. In the book, he expands on this idea by relating a similar theory developed by criminologists James Q. Wilson and George Kelling. Wilson and Kelling applied the same theory to crime-ridden, declining neighborhoods and communities. Wilson, Kelling, Zimbardo and Gladwell all conclude that *chaos is contagious*. Here's an excerpt from Gladwell's book:

"If a window is broken and left unrepaired, people walking by will conclude that no one cares and no one is in charge. Soon, more windows will be broken, and the sense of anarchy will spread from the building to the street on which it faces, sending a signal that anything goes."

There are many applications for this theory. As a person who wants to stay focused, organized and productive, it teaches you to pay close attention to small bits and piles of clutter so they won't become big piles of clutter. *Like chaos, clutter is contagious.*

So What?

It may not seem like a big deal to toss that piece of paper in a stack on the corner of your desk. But stacks turn into piles and piles turn into highly distracting, energy-draining, stress-producing clutter. When things are a mess, you are less likely to care if a few more items are tossed in the piles. If things are in order, you are more likely to keep them that way. In terms of clutter, you *do need to sweat the small stuff*. And it's such an easy step if you want to live an organized, clutter-free life.

Now What?

Here is a simple, two-step solution to help minimize or eliminate clutter:

- Have a designated place to put things.

- Form the habit of putting things away where they belong...in their place.

The steps work well together. People often do not put things away because they do not know where they belong. In this situation, it is usually easier just to toss it somewhere close by. And tossing things somewhere close by creates clutter. The best first step if you want to get rid of clutter is to designate a place to put things...a permanent home. Draw a sketch of all your desk drawers, file cabinets and other storage places. Decide where everything should go and start forming the habit of putting things away when you are not using them.

**Have a place for everything and
put everything in its place.**

15
The Proper Order of Events

What?

How many times have you started to get organized, but for some reason you abandoned the project before you finished the job? You had great intentions and got off to a great start, but the clutter and chaos eventually overwhelmed you and you gave up. This may have happened because you didn't understand the different phases of getting organized or you didn't complete the phases of getting organized in the proper order. Your approach to *getting organized* was *disorganized*.

So What?

One of the main reasons for getting organized is to get *things in order* and establish the habit of *doing the right things* in the *right order*. By approaching your organizing project with the same goals, you will increase your chances of success.

There are four distinct phases of getting organized:

1. Gathering (gather everything that needs to be considered or acted upon)

2. Filtering (get rid of unnecessary items or things that don't matter)

3. Prioritizing (determine the order of importance for your actions)

4. Doing (act on the items in priority order)

It is important to *keep these phases separate* and to *do them in the proper order.* For example, say you have too many things to do and too many things on your mind. Your natural reaction may be to speed up and work harder. A better approach is to slow down and get things under control by methodically going through the four-step process of *gathering, filtering, prioritizing* and *doing.*

If you want to get organized, it is also very important to avoid microfocusing during the four-step process. Microfocusing means getting lost in the details instead of focusing on the larger task. For example, instead of going through *all* the items in your in-box and applying the four-step process above, you stop and start working on the third item you encounter and stop looking at the remaining items. After finishing the third item, you return to the stack and discover the fifth item was more important than the third item. A rookie mistake in the organizing game!

Now What?

Learn to slow down when you feel like speeding up. The typical response to anxiety is action…and action drives out thought. People who do not think about what they are doing usually lose sight of their objectives. In this situation, anxiety escalates and people often respond by redoubling their efforts. They are not getting anywhere, but they are getting there twice as fast. If you are under stress or out of control, it is counterintuitive to slow down and implement this four-step process. Like a race car driver coming in for a pit stop...you don't want to slow down. However, sooner or later even champion racers must stop and take care of critical issues like tires and gas if they want to finish the race. They must slow down when they feel like speeding up. *Gathering, filtering and prioritizing are the equivalent of coming in for a pit stop.*

**Your approach to getting organized
must be organized.**

16
Gathering Incoming Items

What?

Think about how categorizing helps us every day. What if you went to a department store or a grocery store and things were not categorized? What if, instead of grouping like things together, the store manager decided to randomly display the available items? If you needed a particular item, you would have to guess where it might be. If you needed two of the same item, you might find one in the front corner of the store and another mixed up with other unrelated items in the back corner of the store. Life, and shopping, would become a frustrating scavenger hunt. It is just too confusing to display things in a random manner without categorizing them in some way. Think about what it would be like if bookstores, grocery stores or libraries did not use some sort of categorizing systems.

So What?

Most people do not bother to categorize the incoming demands on their time each day. Just like the frustration felt in a store with randomly displayed items, they often feel a loss of control over their workload. Rather than randomly thinking of the multitude of things that compete for your attention each day, place all incoming items in one of five categories:

1. Paper
2. E-mails
3. Voice mails
4. Verbal requests
5. Things you think of that you want to do

It doesn't seem so overwhelming if you reduce the multitude of incoming items into these five simple categories. Develop a system or process to deal with each of these five incoming categories. In the next chapter, we will suggest that there are only five sensible decisions you can make for every incoming item. Five categories of incoming items...five sensible decisions. Handling your workload in this manner not only makes you feel as if you have more control over your life...it actually gives you more control over your life.

Now What?

Stop trying to process incoming items in a random manner. Think of them in terms of the five categories and you are on your way to being a highly organized person.

**Categorizing leads to clarity;
clarity lessens confusion.**

17
The Five Decisions

What?

Learn to convert confusion about what to do with incoming items into one of five sensible decisions. Although it sounds like an insignificant step in the overall process of getting organized, it is a defining moment for people who successfully conquer disorganization. Make one of the following five decisions as soon as possible when you encounter an incoming item:

1. Discard or recycle
2. Delegate
3. Take immediate action
4. Put in a reference file
5. File for follow-up

Making one of these five decisions will be the turning point in your journey from disorganization to organization.

So What?

If you do not have a defined process for dealing with incoming items, you will not get organized. If you do not make your defined process a habit, you will not stay organized. Remember, there are five categories of incoming items: paper, e-mails, voice mails, verbal requests, and things you think of that you want to do. Incoming paper seems to be the most difficult to handle for most people. If you do not have a defined process for dealing with incoming paper, you probably use one of the four following methods to handle it:

1. Stacking
2. Stuffing
3. Spreading
4. A combination of the above three

Think about it. If you do not make one of the five decisions the first time you encounter a piece of paper, it ends up stacked, stuffed or spread out somewhere in your office. It has nowhere else to go! Many courses on getting organized advise you to "handle every piece of paper only once." This is good advice if you are talking about Charmin® or Kleenex® tissues during flu season…but it won't work in the real world. It makes more sense to advise people to "make one of the five decisions" the first time (and every time) you encounter a piece of paper.

Now What?

We will discuss each of the five decisions in the following chapters. It is important that you develop the habit of making one of these five decisions on all incoming items (not just paper) if you want to live a clutter-free life. Getting organized is more about decision-making than cleaning up. You can clean up your office and temporarily get organized, but the clutter will quickly return if you don't have good habits to consistently handle incoming items. Review the following chapters to learn more about these decisions and how they are the building blocks of an overall system to keep you organized.

"Clutter is postponed decisions.®"

— Barbara Hemphill

18
The Five Decisions – Discard

What?

After introducing the five decisions in my training classes, I always ask the participants, "Do I need to explain discard to you?" Most people laugh or chuckle and shake their heads from side to side indicating, "No, you do not need to explain this to us." You would think everyone would have a clear understanding of what is meant by discard. They do seem to have a clear understanding in theory, but somewhere there is a major disconnect when they try to convert theory into action.

So What?

After many years of teaching people how to get organized and visiting their workspaces to help them implement organizing systems, one thing is very clear to me. The habit of discarding unneeded things is the easiest, most effective and *most ignored* step in the organizing process.

Things, especially paper in the form of bills, memos, magazines, newsletters, etc., often *come into your life with little or no effort on your part*. However, and this is a very important point, *they will rarely go out of your life without some effort on your part*. This creates a natural imbalance in your life and in your workspace (or home, car, or any space you control). There you have it! Understand this imbalance and you understand that *you must have a system for moving things out of your life* if you want to avoid being buried in clutter.

If one new piece of paper comes into your life every day and you discard one piece of paper on the same day, your present clutter will remain in equilibrium. However, if 10 new pieces of paper come into your life every day and you only discard one, you will have an additional 3,285 pieces of paper after one year. If 100 new pieces of paper come into your life each day (a conservative estimate for people with fax machines, e-mail systems, customers, bosses, subordinates and co-workers) and you discard none, you will have an additional 36,500 pieces of paper lying around at the end of the year. If you are an executive, forget the 100 new pieces. That's too low an estimate! If you've been in your job for several years without good discarding habits, it's easy to understand why things are a mess.

Now extend this same theory to all the incoming items. Mental clutter is no different than physical clutter. It's just cluttering up the space between your ears instead of your workspace.

Now What?

Let's put this all in perspective. The total surface area of the Earth is approximately 197,000,000 square miles or 5,492,044,800,000,000 square feet (509,600,000 square kilometers for the non-USA readers). The average office workspace is 80 to 150 square feet. Maybe yours is bigger, say up to 600 to 700 square feet if you are the big boss. Come on...how big a deal is it for you to keep up with your 80 to 700 square feet? Try these two simple ideas. Have a serious throwaway session! Don't bother trying to organize things you shouldn't be keeping in the first place. Then, get in the habit of throwing more pieces of paper out than you let come in your office every day. Now do the same for all the incoming items...both mental and physical.

Discover the joy of throwing things away!
Learn to let go. Especially let go of things that are
associated with negative feelings and experiences.

19
The Five Decisions – Delegate

What?

If you were walking alone down a street and saw a $100 bill on the ground, would you pick it up? Or would you just walk on by and leave it there? I'm not asking this question to test your ethics. We'll assume it was just dropped on the ground and there is no hope of finding the owner. Most of you would pick it up and get a little rush; a feeling that it's your lucky day. The skill of delegation is just like that $100 bill lying on the ground, and many of you walk right by it and leave it untouched.

So What?

People frequently tell me, "I know I should delegate more. I just don't do it for some reason." If they studied the true reasons people do not delegate, they might reconsider making such a statement. Psychologists believe people do not delegate for the following reasons:

- They don't know how (a form of managerial incompetence).

- They are control freaks (they can't let go of anything).

- They don't trust others (often because they feel they can't personally be trusted).

- They have an unhealthy need for power and domination.

- They don't know how to teach and develop people (another version of incompetence).

- They lack humility (they think they always can do things better than anyone).

The reasons go on and on, but none are very flattering. By the way, the socially acceptable versions of these reasons aren't worded like any of the above examples. These excuses go something like this:

- I just don't have time right now.

- This is very important. I want to take care of it myself.

- I'm not sure my staff is ready to take that on yet.

- I've got to make sure this is done right.

It's usually not a matter of delegating or not delegating. Everyone must do some delegating to survive. Everyone can't make their own bread, fix their own car, and carry their own mail to the recipient. Likewise, people can't delegate everything or they are no longer necessary. The quest is to get better at delegation and delegate when it is appropriate.

Now What?

First, recognize that there are people who are better at certain things than you are. Even though you may hold a higher title, they are just flat-out better than you and that is okay. Rely on them to help you. It is a sign of strength to ask for help when it makes sense. It is a sign of weakness to refuse help when you need it. Second, there are people at work who are not as good as you in certain areas and you have been given the responsibility to teach them what you know (it's called leadership and management). Unless you are absolutely the last stop on the delegation train at work…offload as much as you can so you can work on more important things. Start delegating more today.

Maybe now when you say, "I know I should delegate more. I just don't do it for some reason.", or you demonstrate that same message through your actions, you will understand that some of your co-workers – who know the real reasons people don't delegate – just learned something very unflattering about you.

Teaching and sharing your knowledge is a noble endeavor. People who know how to delegate are great teachers.

20
The Five Decisions – Take Immediate Action

What?

How many times have you put off something several times and when you finally got around to doing it…it only took a minute or two to complete? So far, we've suggested that you discard or delegate everything possible. But what if you can't discard or delegate it and it will only take a minute or two to complete? In this case, do it when you first encounter it!

So What?

We all have those items that we can do quickly, read quickly, review and initial or sign, approve, etc. For many of you, opening mail is a great example of this. When you focus on the process of opening the mail, you can go through a huge stack in a short time. The alternative is to let it pile up and look at it later. The second you make the decision to let anything pile up, you are headed back to stacking, stuffing or spreading. In short, you are generating clutter. Here's the bottom line on the relationship between clutter and productivity:

- The key to improving productivity is improving concentration.

- The key to improving concentration is minimizing distractions.

- Clutter is distracting.

The word "clotter" is not used very much these days. You can still find this word if you can find a copy of Webster's 1913 dictionary. The word clutter comes from the word clotter. Clotter means to clot or get stuck. Think of your incoming items as you would blood cells flowing through your body. It's not a good thing when they become clotted. Blood clots will quickly wreak havoc with your circulatory system. Not taking immediate action on items that can be done in a very short time will quickly wreak havoc with your organizing system.

Now What?

Go with the flow! Keep the short-term tasks moving through your office and life.

"You can pay me now, or you can pay me later!"
— Advice from a personified FRAM® Oil Filter

21

The Five Decisions – Put in a Reference File

What?

Reference file items are incoming items you want to keep for some reason, but no further action is required on the items at the present time. These are memos, articles and other documents that you may want to refer to later. The key question with these items is, "How can I find them when I need them?"

So What?

In school, students often vote on who is "most likely to succeed" or "most likely to do this or that." If we conducted a similar contest for incoming items, reference file items would be voted "most likely to become clutter." Some studies show that you will never use or refer to up to 80 percent of the items in your file cabinets. The good news is at least they made it to your file cabinets and are not cluttering your workspace. The truth is, you may refer to some of these items and it is okay to keep things that you think you may need later...*if you can find them when you need them*. However, if you do not have a filing system that allows you to easily retrieve filed items, you are wasting your time and money hanging on to these items.

Now What?

As mentioned previously in this book, I personally think a software product called Taming the Paper Tiger® is one of the best solutions to this problem. But any system that allows you to quickly find things in your files will work. Here are a few tips on reference filing for those of you who want to continue using manual filing systems:

- Categorize your files into broad categories so you don't have to search through all your files when you are looking for an item. For example, use separate drawers for customers, administrative items, product information, personal information, etc.

- Use nouns as the lead word on your labels, if possible. For example, instead of labeling a file "New Prospects" and filing it under the "N" category, label it "Prospects, New" and file it under the "P" category.

- Don't think of where you should put it when you are labeling the file as much as how will you find it in six months or a year?

- If you don't have someone to prepare reference files for you, put them in one place and file several of them at once. Don't stop working to set up individual reference files. Do stop and put away reference files at least once a week so they will not build up and become clutter.

- If you like your file labels printed, use Avery® labels and templates to create them.

- In some cases, it makes more sense to put reference items in binders rather than file drawers.

- Purge your files at least once a year. Divide the number of files you have into the number of working days for the month, and go through a few files a day for a month rather than trying to do it all at once (you may find a lot of things you have been looking for when you do this).

Whatever you decide, have some kind of system that helps you find things when you need them. If it works for you, it's a good system.

Studies indicate that people spend 30 minutes to two hours a day looking for things in their office.

22

The Five Decisions – File for Follow-up

What?

A follow-up item is an incoming item you must *personally* take some sort of follow-up action on. At this point, you should have already considered four other decisions that didn't accurately describe what you should do with this item...you cannot discard it, delegate it, take immediate action on it or reference file it. Since you are not going to take immediate action on the item, but you are eventually going to take action on it, you must put it somewhere until you find the time to work on it. We will show you exactly where to put these items in the chapter on follow-up files. For now, just remember this is one of your five choices if you want to stay organized.

So What?

I've seen many people get stuck on follow-up items. In the case of paper (such as going through mail or an in-box), people pick up an item and stare at it. They can't seem to quickly decide what to do with it, so their gathering process bogs down. The primary cause – they start trying to think too much about what to *eventually* do with it. Don't overthink it. Remember, you are gathering things in this phase of getting organized. If you over-think decisions at this point, you are shifting out of the gathering phase of getting organized and into the doing phase (jumping over the filtering and prioritizing steps altogether). It's not time to start doing yet. At this point, the question is… "Which one of the five decisions is it?" You must train your brain to ask this question the first time you encounter an incoming item or you will get bogged down.

The file for follow-up step does require more thought than the first four decisions. With the first four decisions, the next action is self-explanatory…you discard it, delegate it, take immediate action or file it. However, once you decide an incoming item is a follow-up item, you need to ask two additional questions:

1. What is the next thing I need to do with this item?

2. When will I do it?

It is hard to answer the "when" question if you don't know the answer to the "what" question.

Now What?

Here's the drill with follow-up items:

1. Ask "What is the next step (in general, not in detail)?"

2. Ask "When will I work on the next step?"

3. Put it in the appropriate tickler file (to be explained in a later chapter).

If a follow-up item is not in paper form, quickly convert it to paper. Although it sounds a bit old-fashioned to convert voice mails, verbal requests, and things you think of that you want to do to paper, it makes the most sense for most people. Why convert everything to paper? Most incoming items are already in paper form and others can be easily converted. For example, e-mails are easy to convert by printing out the first page to use as a reminder. *When you get ready to prioritize your work, it is important to have everything you plan to do for a given period of time in one place and in one form.* The time it takes to convert a follow-up item to paper will be easily offset when you learn to prioritize your work in 60 seconds or less (see Chapter 34).

If you can't discard it, delegate it, take immediate action on it or file it for future reference ...it is a follow-up item.

23
Control Point Drawer

What?

It's right there! Within a few feet (or possibly inches) of your desktop is one of the most productivity-enhancing devices you can find. This simple tool for keeping your life in order has been hidden in plain sight from most of you for years. It's the common, ordinary, garden-variety hanging file drawer. This often-ignored item can easily be converted into a productivity-boosting, air traffic control point drawer. Instead of using this drawer to control airplanes circling and waiting to land, we will use it to control papers and tasks that are circling in your life...waiting to land on your desk.

So What?

There are several chapters about how to effectively use hanging files in this book. But in order to effectively use hanging files, you have to have a place to hang them. As in real estate, the key to success in filing is...location, location, location. Here's a profound fact. You will be more likely to do something if it is easy to do. Therefore, since I am going to suggest that you reach into hanging files several times a day to manage your workflow, it needs to be easy to reach them. That's why the control point drawer needs to be no more than a swivel away...not a swivel and a roll. Pick the most convenient drawer. If you are right-handed, it is probably the hanging file drawer on the right side of your desk. Use this file drawer to keep up with the daily incoming items that compete for your time and attention.

Now What?

Here are the files that I suggest you set up at a minimum in your control point drawer:

- A set of files labeled "1" to "31"
- A set of files labeled "January" to "December"
- One file labeled "Follow-up Forms"
- One file for your boss
- One file for your spouse or significant other (if you have one)
- A *separate* labeled file for *each* ongoing meeting that you attend on a regular basis (e.g., "Staff Meeting," "Management Meeting" or "Sales Meeting")
- One file labeled "Casual Reading"
- One file labeled "Waiting on Response"
- One file labeled "Purchases/Errands"

There is a separate chapter in this book on how to use each of these files. Even if you never use them, *you'll look much more organized* to your boss and co-workers. Even the most highly organized, methodical people will gather around and *ooh* and *ah* when they see your control point drawer.

Other chapters will give you pointers on how to effectively and efficiently use this drawer. However, it is important that you understand that nothing is permanently filed in this drawer. You will use this as a place to keep items until you need them. And that is one of the key issues in getting and staying organized...being able to find things when you need them. Take a moment now to set up your own personal control point drawer, then read all the chapters on "files" in this book. You will see how handy this little drawer can be.

**Hanging files were here before you were born.
Many timesaving gadgets to help you at work have
come and gone...hanging files are still here.**

24
Files – Labeled "1" to "31"

What?

Years ago, after dinosaurs roamed the Earth, but before electronic gadgets evolved and proliferated, people often set up tickler files to help them remember to do things. One of the simplest systems involved the use of old-fashioned hanging files labeled "1" to "31." People who used these files understood that there were no more than 31 days in any month. Therefore, if they wanted to remember to follow up on an item on the 15th of the month, they would simply drop a reminder in the file labeled "15." Then, they simply formed the habit of looking in the files each day to remind them of what needed to be done for that day. If they planned to follow up on an item on the 23rd of the month, a note would be dropped in the file labeled "23," and so on and so on.

So What?

When I show the 1 to 31 files to many of my older class participants, they often tell me, "I used a system like that years ago." I ask them, "Did it work for you?" They usually reply, "Yep, it worked fine." When I ask, "Why did you quit using it?" They usually reply, "I don't know."

I found that many of these people got caught in the latest gadget trap. Years ago, a wise person told me, "The true test of a gadget, computer or piece of software is... *'Is it easier than a pencil?'* " I have expanded this wisdom to include more universal applications by restating it as follows: *Is it easier than something that is already working quite well?* Don't get me wrong. I am not a Luddite. I love gadgets, computers and digital toys. But not if they don't work better than a pencil...or something that is already serving me well.

Now What?

If you followed the instructions in the previous chapter on setting up a control point drawer, you have already set up 1 to 31 files. If not, now is the time to do it. Here's a rather strong statement. A set of hanging files labeled "1" to "31" can serve as the core...the most vital element...of an organized person's life. As you will read in Chapter 34 ("Prioritizing Your Workload"), using a set of 1 to 31 files allows you to prioritize your daily work in 60 seconds or less. No other system I know of makes it so easy to keep up with things and prioritize things so quickly. Many other uses of hanging files will be discussed in this book. When you use them together, you will be amazed at how much they can help you improve your ability to focus, organize and prioritize.

The latest gadget or invention is not necessarily the best gadget or invention.

25
Files – Labeled "January" to "December"

What?

Everyone in every organization has one of three follow-up reputations...*sometimes, always* or *never*. You know the three types well. The "sometimes" people are hit or miss. *Sometimes* they follow up, *sometimes* they don't. The "always" people are totally reliable. You can *always* count on them to do what they say they will do. They *always* produce high-quality work and *always* get their work done on time. And then there are the "never" people. They *never* get anything done on time. They *never* follow up. They *never* return phone calls. You can *never* rely on them.

So What?

It is hard to meet your deadlines if the people that work for you and support you do not meet their deadlines. January to December hanging files help you accomplish two important things. They help *you* improve *your* follow-up reputation and they help you improve how well *other people* follow up on their commitments to you.

Now What?

Set up 12 new files in the control point drawer as discussed in Chapter 23. Label the files from January through December.

Since you will not reach into these files as frequently as the 1 to 31 files, drop them in the file drawer behind the 1 to 31 files that you previously set up.

Now, if you talk to a client in March and they ask you to call them back in mid-September, you have a system to help you remember this request. Immediately after the call, simply fill out a follow-up form (see Chapter 26) and drop it in the hanging file labeled "September." Six months later, on the last working day of August, pull the contents from the September file and decide when you will follow up on all the items you have dropped in the file during the year. In the example above, you might look at your calendar and make sure the 15th of September is a working day for you. If so, drop the follow-up form in the 1 to 31 file labeled "15." On the morning of the 15th, you will pull this follow-up form out of the hanging file and be reminded to call the client. If you need more time to prepare for the call, drop it in the file for the 13th or 14th. By handling follow-up items in this manner, you will not only remove a lot of clutter from your desktop...you will remove the clutter from your mind. Let the January to December files serve as your long-term memory.

If you let other people miss your deadline once, they will be more likely to ignore your future deadlines. Therefore, use the January to December files to keep them on track. When you delegate a project or task, use these files and a follow-up form to establish check-in dates for the project. Let's say it is February and you delegate a project that is not due until December. After assigning the project to another person, jot their name and a few words to remind you of the project on a follow-up form. Then drop the completed form in the monthly file halfway between the present date and the due date. In this case, you would drop the form in the July hanging file. When July rolls around, you will see the form and be reminded of the project. Call the person working on the project and say, "I was just thinking of the project we discussed in February. How is it going?" You will get one of two responses. The person working on the project may respond with solid details on the status of the project and demonstrate that they are clearly on top of things. In this case, you may just move the follow-up form closer to the due date and follow up as necessary. However, when you ask about the status of the project, you may hear a long silent pause...then the other person will say, "Oh yeah, don't worry about it, everything is going great." You get no facts, no details and no comfort that the project is on track. If you get this response, you might move the follow-up reminder forward a week or so and call again. After you call two or three times to check up on the project, most people will realize that you are serious about getting the job done on time.

It has been my experience that with some people, you rarely have to follow up. They have an "always" follow-up reputation without your help. You might put the reminder in a day or two before the project is due just to give both of you a little recovery time in case unexpected, last minute issues arise. However, with some people (the "never" follow-up crowd), you might need to move the form forward a week at a time and keep bugging them to make sure the job gets done on time. Use this simple system to improve your own follow-up reputation and the follow-up reputations of those who support you. January to December files also come in handy for helping you remember birthdays, anniversaries and other important events. Give them a try. I'm sure you will think of lots of ways to use the January to December files to improve your follow-up reputation.

Good luck on becoming an "always."

26
Files – Follow-up Forms

What?

Did you know as you get older you start to forget things more often? For example, you might be sitting in your office, thinking of something you need in another room. You get up and go to the other place and suddenly realize...*I can't remember why I came to this place.* I call it the "supply closet hereafter syndrome." You go to the supply closet to get something and just stand there, with a puzzled look on your face, trying desperately to remember what you are "here after."

So What?

It gets worse! There will come a day when you will call someone. Get this straight...*you called them.* After one or two rings you get that sinking feeling and you think, *"Who was I calling? I hope they answer with their name."* You were safe in the old days. You could just hang up and breathe a sigh of relief. Unfortunately, caller ID now keeps you from hiding many of these senior moments. And senior moments seem to be occurring at a younger and younger age. With so much to remember to plan, and so much to remember to do, and so much to remember to follow up on, it's getting more difficult every day to keep track of everything going on in our lives.

Now What?

When you find yourself staring at the supply closet wondering why you are there...grab a hanging file. Label the hanging file "Follow-up Forms" and fill it with blank follow-up forms. You can easily make your own format for these forms on any word processing program and then make multiple copies on the copy machine (if you can remember where the copy machine is and how to use it). Most people include a place for names, dates, comments, contact information, etc. Actually, you can use blank sheets of paper if you prefer. My follow-up forms file is the first hanging file in my control point drawer (see Chapter 23). I keep 25 or 30 blank forms in the file at any given time. When you think of things you need to follow up on, pull out a form and jot down enough information to remind you to follow up on the item. These are also great for keeping up with those otherwise undocumented verbal requests.

By the way, don't use tiny notes, sticky notes or other small pieces of paper as follow-up forms. For example, if someone hands you one of those pink phone messages and asks you to follow up on it, staple it to a full-sized sheet of paper or to one of your follow-up forms before you put it in the appropriate follow-up file. Small pieces of paper tend to get lost in the bottom of hanging files.

**There are three sure signs you are getting old.
One, you start to forget things,
two...I can't remember the other two.**

27
Files – People

What?

As you go through the new items in your in-box one morning, you see something you need to discuss with your boss. You spontaneously jump up and head toward the boss's office. You walk in her door and ask, "Have you got a minute?" She looks slightly frustrated. You've done it again! You have interrupted your workflow, your boss's workflow and probably a few other people's workflow between your office and the boss's office. We will assume you have a tolerant boss. Even though she is busy, she stops whatever she is doing and gives you her full attention. You resolve the issue, return to your office and continue going through your in-box. Guess what? Two items farther down in the stack, you see another item that you need to discuss with your boss. Off you go again...headed to the boss's office. This time, she looks more than slightly frustrated. "What is it now?" she asks.

So What?

First of all, it is not a good idea to constantly interrupt your boss. It's a better idea to be somewhat selective about what you take to a higher level. Unless the person who hired you is a control freak, they should expect you to take care of as many issues as possible without their help. Otherwise, they don't need you. Learn to develop a sense of appropriateness about what you take to your boss. And in all circumstances, try to avoid constantly interrupting people above, below or beside you on the organizational chart.

Now What?

Set up a hanging file labeled "Boss" or label it with the name of your boss. Then go through your entire in-box before you get up from your chair. By the time you get to the bottom, you may have four or five items to discuss with your boss. Now call her and say, "I've got five things I need to discuss with you and I think it will take about 30 minutes. What time is best for you?" Much of the time people waste each day comes from having to deal with interruptions. We rarely get enough uninterrupted time to concentrate and focus on our true priorities. If you were the boss, wouldn't you like it if all your direct reports set up a boss file and used it to give you more uninterrupted time? If you would like it, then consider doing it for your boss.

Use the same idea to help you keep up with things to discuss with your spouse or significant other. How many times have you been doing something at work and thought of something you wanted to discuss? However, by the time you talk to them, you have forgotten what you wanted to tell them. Set up a spouse file. When you think of things to discuss with your spouse, jot it on a note and drop it in the spouse file. If your spouse calls during the day, grab the contents of the file. After your spouse's issues have been discussed, you can go over your issues with them. At the end of the day, you can check the file to see if you need to discuss any issues with them when you get home.

Be careful and limit the use of people files. Some people get excited about this idea and decide to set up a lot of people files. For example, if they have six people reporting to them, they set up a file for each of their direct reports, their boss and their spouse. Remember, we are trying to keep things simple. The fewer files you must monitor daily, the easier it will be to stay on top of them. You do not want to be constantly monitoring eight files to make sure you haven't forgotten somebody. For that reason, I suggest you only use this idea for your boss and your spouse. If it is a follow-up item related to one of your direct reports or anyone else, put the item in the appropriate 1 to 31 file, just like any other follow-up item. Using people files will make you look more organized, feel more organized and be more organized. Hanging files typically cost 25 cents each or less. You will get a very good return on your investment on this 50-cent idea.

Only interrupt people who are focused on their own agenda as a last resort.

28
Files – Meetings

What?

During my training classes, I always ask the participants, "How many of you still have ongoing meetings that you must attend on a weekly or monthly basis?" That's when I usually hear a lot of groans from the audience. It seems as if the periodic "show-and-tell" meetings are alive and well in corporate America.

So What?

Rather than considering these little get-togethers a waste of your time, use the meetings to learn about the power of understanding different perspectives. When you go from making sure *your* point of view on an issue is "the one that gets the most attention," to seeing a project or problem *through the eyes of others*, you are headed in the right direction.

I recently heard Steve Connor of Synergy Development Associates explain the term "perspective" in a unique way. Steve told us to imagine we were in a room across from a huge ball that was painted red on one side and white on the other side. We were sitting where we could see both sides, but two individuals standing on opposite sides of the ball could only see one side. If you asked the two people standing on opposite sides to describe the color of the ball, you would likely get two very different answers. The person on one side of the ball would say it is red, the person on the opposite side would say it is white. Which one is right? Think of how many problems exist in your company, your life and the world because red and white thinkers insist they are seeing things clearly...they are right...but they're only seeing things from their perspective. In the ball example, you would be in the best position to interpret reality from your perspective...half the ball is red and half the ball is white. The more you understand that people naturally have different perspectives, and how to recognize why they have different perspectives, the more successful you will be at work and in life.

Now What?

Set up a hanging file for each of the ongoing meetings you must attend. How many times have you forgotten to bring up an issue at one of these meetings? Put reminders in the files to help you remember anything you want to discuss. However, also put in a reminder to learn something new about the different perspectives of the people in the meeting. If you are meeting with these people on an ongoing basis, they are probably important to your success. The more you know about their point of view, the more effective you will be when interacting with them. Listen carefully to their point of view and try to understand the beliefs that drive their behavior. It's actually a lot of fun to ask questions and try to figure out what makes them tick. You might as well use these meetings to have fun and learn how to better understand your co-workers.

> **"Unless they share our opinions,
> we seldom find people sensible."**
> — La Rochefoucauld

29
Files – Casual Reading

What?

Here's some good news. For those of you that have "guilt stacks" of unread magazines, newspapers, newsletters and other miscellaneous piles of reading material laying around your office...the world is not going to come to an end if you never read these stacks.

So What?

Give yourself a break! Consider throwing the current piles away and starting over with reasonable reading goals.

Now What?

From now on, start separating everything you plan to read into two categories...the "have to read" stuff and the "would like to read" stuff. Put the items that fall into the first category in your 1 to 31 files on the day you plan to read them. Schedule time to read these like you would schedule time for any other task. It is part of everybody's job to keep up with current events and look for new ideas to improve their jobs or businesses. Many people think this is strictly "take-home" work to be done after regular working hours. If you like to read at home...fine. But if you would prefer to spend more time with your family or on your hobbies...do your work reading at work.

For the "would like to read" items, put them in a file labeled "Casual Reading" and save them for those times when you are waiting for something else to happen, or looking for something to do to occupy unexpected (or expected) downtime. Take the file with you anytime you think you may have to wait on someone or something. Here are some examples:

- Airplane trips
- Car trips when someone else is driving
- Commuting time on trains, in taxis, etc.
- Waiting for a meeting to begin
- Waiting for an appointment with the doctor or dentist
- Waiting to pick up your kids
- Time off recovering from a heart attack because you pushed yourself too hard

If you really want to increase the odds that you will actually read the items in the casual reading file, use the *rip-and-read* technique. On the first day you get a magazine or newspaper, rip out the articles you plan to read. Put these ripped-out or clipped-out articles in your casual reading file. They will be more digestible and you will be more likely to read them. By the way, if you do your periodical reading at the public library or at a bookstore or newsstand, they do not like the rip-and-read idea. Use your good judgment if you don't actually own the magazine.

During my regular workday, I frequently rip out articles or print out e-mails and put them in my casual reading file. Anytime I leave my office, I grab the contents of the casual reading file and put it in my briefcase just in case I find myself with a few minutes to spare between events. You'll be surprised at how many of the "would like to read" items you can knock out if you use this idea.

Here's one more tip: If you receive a current issue of a magazine and you have not opened last month's issue, do not proceed with life until you glance at last month's magazine and apply the rip-and-read technique. Let the new issue be the trigger event...the ultimate deadline...to remind you that you are getting behind in your reading. If you go more than two months without opening a magazine and the next issue shows up, cancel the magazine and use the money you save to invest in a speed-reading course.

Unread magazines turn into unnecessary clutter.

30
Files – Waiting for Response

What?

Sometimes you need a place to temporarily park papers or files while you are waiting for a response from another person. Park them somewhere you can immediately find them when needed.

So What?

How many times have you been working on a project, making good progress and you suddenly needed information from someone else before you can continue? Then you call the other person and get their voice mail. Rats…you are stuck! You need a good place to put the items related to this project until the other person returns your call.

Now What?

Put all the items related to your project in a file folder and drop it in a file labeled "Waiting for Response." That way, you will know exactly where it is when the other person returns your call. Remember, this file is not a permanent filing place. It is a temporary holding file for daily pending items. If the person calls back the same day, retrieve the folder from the file and record the information needed to continue your progress on the project. If they have not returned your call toward the end of the day, call them again or put the file in the 1 to 31 file for the next day to remind you to follow up. Try not to let anything sit too long in this file. Remember, you teach what you allow. Failure to follow up on your part may send a signal to the other person that they can continue to ignore your requests in the future.

**Develop a reputation for always following up
...and following up will get easier.**

31
Other Files to Help You Follow Up

What?

We have discussed several follow-up files that can be used by most people. Also, set up files in your control point drawer that are unique to your situation.

So What?

If you must follow up on something on an ongoing basis, set up a file to store information and reminders related to the item. For example, you may teach a Sunday school class or go to a night course. You will occasionally think of something related to the class during your workday. Jot down your thought on a piece of paper and drop it in the appropriate file. Knowing where to find something when you need it is the important issue...not trying to remember everything. Hanging file folders are cheap. When in doubt, set one up and try it for a while. See if it helps you follow up. If not, get rid of it or recycle it.

Now What?

Here are a few suggestions for additional follow-up files:

- Purchases/Errands file
- Phone List file

- Calendar file
- Blank Pad of Paper file
- Someday/Maybe file (for ideas you are considering)
- Gift Idea file
- Tax Receipts file

Set up any files that work for you. Just don't cram your control point drawer so full of files that you can't get in and out of it easily.

"Never memorize something that you can look up."

— Albert Einstein

32
Capturing Incoming Items

What?

One of the main benefits of getting more organized is the feeling that you have reasonable control over all the things you need or want to do. A good capturing system for incoming items is just as good as having a good memory. Without one, you will never get the feeling that you have things under control.

So What?

In the Old West, cowboys would round up their cows or horses and drive them in herds across the range. Occasionally, they would have to chase after strays wandering away from the herd. No self-respecting cowpoke would allow strays to wander too far away from the herd or out of their sight. If they couldn't maintain control over their part of the herd, they would be branded a greenhorn and laughed at around the nightly campfire.

Capturing and controlling your incoming items is similar to rounding up the herd. Your strays are in the form of sticky notes, little pieces of paper or things you never wrote down anywhere. You will never get that warm and fuzzy feeling that you have everything under control until you develop a good capturing system. And it's not just your work issues. How many times has someone told you about a great book, movie or restaurant and you forgot about it because you didn't write it down anywhere?

Now What?

One of the best ways to capture incoming items is by simply writing them down on 3-by-5 index cards. Keep a few cards with you all the time and get in the habit of writing each item on a separate card. Since they are portable, require no batteries and will easily fit in a pocket, they are great for capturing things when you are away from your office. When you return to your office, you can make one of the five decisions on each card and decide what to do with it next. If it is a follow-up item that needs to go in your 1 to 31 files, staple it to a full-size sheet of paper and put it in the appropriate file.

You can also use a small portable tape recorder to capture these items, but you will look like a nerd if you go around talking into your tape recorder all the time. That's okay – if your self-esteem is high enough. Looking like a nerd is a small price to pay to help you stay organized. Recorders are great for the things you suddenly remember when you are in the car going 70 miles per hour down the highway.

If it is something you want to remember or follow up on, get in the habit of writing it down as soon as you hear it or think of it. Any good organizing system starts with a good capturing system. Don't allow important items to fall through the cracks of your memory.

To err is human, to forget, routine.

33
Backfilling Your 1 to 31 Files

What?

If you plan to do something on a certain day next month and that day has already passed this month, should you put it in next month's file or the appropriate 1 to 31 file? I suggest you always put items like this in the file for the next month and transfer it to the appropriate 1 to 31 file on the last working day of the current month.

So What?

Let's say it is the 20th of May and you are going through your in-box. You pick up an item and make the decision that it is a follow-up item for the 8th of June. At this point, should you put the item in the 1 to 31 file labeled "8," or should you put it in the monthly file labeled "June"? I know we are getting into a rather picky question here, but I get this question fairly often during my seminars. I am always impressed when I do. It's a sign that people are really thinking through how they will use the system.

Now What?

I suggest you put the item described above in the June file. On the last working day of May, you can pull all the items out of the

June file and transfer them to the appropriate day in June. In this example, if you backfill your files (put items in files representing days of the month that have already passed), you may lose confidence in your filing system. You will see items in the files for days that have already passed and not know if they are for next month, or if they are forgotten current month items. Other people solve this problem by rolling the files forward after the day has passed. On the 8th of the month, they physically pick up the file labeled "8" and put it at the back of their daily files. Their files are now in their control point drawer with files 9 through 31 followed by files 1 through 8. Use the technique that works best for you.

**Don't be afraid to ask dumb questions.
They're easier to handle than dumb mistakes.**

34
Prioritizing Your Workload

What?

Prioritizing is all about deciding what should be done next and doing one thing at a time. In order to prioritize your workload, you must put things in order of importance. Chaos will happen on its own with or without your assistance. Prioritizing will only happen if you have a system for making sure it happens.

So What?

Assigning equal weight to the order of importance is a good idea if you are talking about your children. It's not a good idea when you are trying to decide what to do next at work. Prioritizing is one of those times in life when it is okay to play favorites. As the old saying goes, "When everything is a priority, nothing is a priority." If you think prioritizing your workload is difficult, imagine what it must be like for emergency room physicians during a major disaster trying to prioritize incoming patients. They must use a process called "triage" to prioritize their activities.

Although the concept of triage has been around for quite a while, most of us were introduced to this technique in the popular TV series *M.A.S.H.* Triage is a French word meaning to "sort" or "choose." When Hawkeye and the other members of the surgical unit were flooded with incoming patients, they used a technique called triage to determine who would get the benefit of their limited resources. Incoming patients were quickly sorted into three categories:

1. Patients who will not survive, even with treatment.

2. Patients who will survive without treatment.

3. Patients who will not survive without immediate treatment.

The patients who would not survive without immediate treatment were given immediate attention, and other patients were only allocated resources after these patients were treated and stabilized. It is a short metaphorical jump from a M.A.S.H. unit to your business and your life. Learn from Hawkeye and his gang of true professionals, and allocate your limited time and energy to things that really matter. Everyone seems to talk about the importance of prioritizing, but few people seem to be doing it on a consistent basis.

Now What?

If you have established the habit of using the 1 to 31 files described in Chapter 24, prioritizing will be easy for you. In most cases, you can now prioritize your work in 60 seconds or less. At the end of each day, simply pull the contents of the next day's file. Each piece of paper or folder in the file should represent one project or task you plan to work on tomorrow. Lay all the items on your desktop so you can see each of them individually. Now perform triage on the items. Pick up the item that is most important and place it facedown on your desk. Now pick up the next most important item and place it facedown on top of the first item. Keep doing this until all the items are facedown in one stack. Now turn the stack faceup. You now have your work in priority order. Place all the papers in your next day's 1 to 31 file and go home. When you return the next day, pull out the item that was on the top of the stack and totally focus on it until you complete your work on it. Then tackle the next item, and so forth and so on.

Knowing what to do is often not as important as knowing what to do next.

35
Prioritizing Your Workload – Special Situations

What?

Wouldn't it be nice if everything always went as smoothly as described in the previous chapter? Using a good organizing system, you should have many well-planned, highly productive days. However, we all know that no matter how organized you are, you still occasionally have too much to do or too many unexpected events that throw you offtrack.

So What?

If you are a human being working on the planet Earth, you can expect the following to occasionally happen:

- You will have too much work to accomplish in the amount of time you have to accomplish it.

- You will get interrupted when you are trying to focus on your most important issue.

- You will have to go to a run-on meeting that takes longer than you planned.

- You will not be able to go to work because you are sick or you have a sick child.

Now What?

In general, avoid hard scheduling (putting appointments on your calendar) more than 50 percent of your day. Interruptions, unscheduled meetings and unexpected events are a way of life in most companies, so it is better to be realistic at the beginning of the day than frustrated at the end of the day. Remember, you can always begin working on the items in tomorrow's 1 to 31 file if you are lucky enough to finish all the items you had planned for today.

- If after you prioritize your work, you realize you are overloaded for the day, pull items from the bottom of your prioritized stack and rethink them. The items on the bottom should be your lowest priorities. See if you can eliminate them, delegate them or postpone them. Admit that you cannot do everything in your stack. It will help reduce the guilt feelings later.

- If you get interrupted, quickly ask the person what they want. There are two possibilities:

  1. What they want is *more important* than what you are working on. This happens in the real world. Put your work away, give them your full attention and deal with the issue. Get back to work on your priorities as soon as possible.

  2. What they want is *not as important* as what you are working on. Ask them to get back with you after you have finished with your own priorities.

- If you have a run-on meeting that takes longer than you anticipated, reset your priorities as soon as you return to your office. In this situation, new incoming items may have appeared in your in-box, on your desktop or on your chair while you were in the meeting. Make one of the five decisions we discussed in an earlier chapter on each of the new incoming items and reprioritize your work. This is the equivalent of having a "human reset button." Using the system we have described, it is so easy to reset you can do it anytime you feel things are getting out of control.

- If you cannot make it to work for some reason, call a co-worker and ask them to pull the contents of your follow-up file for the day. This will allow you to easily redirect any items that need prompt attention.

Learn to expect the unexpected. But don't allow other people to put their priorities ahead of yours. Look for ways to keep your priorities on track. Unless you are a very senior executive with a full-time person responsible for your schedule, no one else is likely to do this for you.

**"Our greatest weariness
comes from work not done."**

— Eric Hoffer

36
One Thing at a Time

What?

As mentioned earlier, the closest some people ever get to being highly organized is the day before they go on vacation. That's the time when many people finally buckle down, get focused and get important things done. They don't want to go on vacation with a lot of unfinished business hanging over their heads. When they walk out of their office that day, they feel great. It is one of the few times they have their workload under control.

So What?

Let's assume for a moment that it is time for you to go on vacation. There are other lessons to be learned as you head out on your journey.

Assume you are headed down the road in your car. The vehicle is running smoothly, the kids are in the back behaving, and you are headed down the interstate slightly above the speed limit. Just fast enough for the state troopers to leave you alone. There are five lanes and traffic is moving along nicely. Your stress is quickly evaporating. You are escaping the gravitational force of city traffic and are headed to the beach for a week of fun and relaxation. Suddenly, you look ahead and see some orange barrels. Then you see a road sign that says, "One Lane – One Mile Ahead." In this situation, does everybody politely get in line and prepare to merge into the single lane? No! They go around you on the left and on the right...racing to the front of the line...jamming traffic, creating a huge mess and causing your anxiety to return. But something interesting happens when you pass that last orange barrel that forces you into a single lane. *You start making steady progress.* You may not be going as fast as you'd like, but your stress level is decreasing because all the traffic has merged and you are steadily moving forward. It is odd that the people a mile behind you are fighting chaos with *five available lanes* and you are making steady progress with *one lane*.

Now What?

That is exactly what is happening to you when you allow the five incoming items: paper, e-mails, voice mails, verbal requests and things you think of, to jam up your day. You end up in the middle of chaos. Learn to keep things in "one lane." Focus on making steady progress rather than allowing the five incoming items to overwhelm you. Everyone has to juggle tasks occasionally. But if you find yourself doing it too often, it's time to get everything in one lane and focus on one thing at a time.

Stop trying to multitask! It is not a good thing to do. Focus on the most important thing you have to do...get closure on it...and then move on to the next most important task and give it your full and undivided attention.

37
The Overloaded and Confused Cycle

What?

One normal by-product of disorganization is the overloaded and confused cycle. When we begin to get overloaded, we begin to get confused. Typically we ask, "What should I do next when there seems to be so many things to do?" However, incoming items do not stop showing up just because we are overloaded and confused. They keep right on coming, making the situation worse...leading to more overloading and more confusion. There are both ineffective and effective ways to handle being overloaded and confused. Choosing effective responses can slow down and eventually stop the escalating cycle.

So What?

We all get overloaded at times. Learn to quickly recognize the feelings that signal you are getting overloaded such as anxiety and confusion. Then learn how to effectively respond and keep the overloaded and confused cycle from escalating.

Now What?

Here are some *ineffective* responses to being overloaded:

- Procrastinating

- Substituting unproductive action (overeating, over-drinking, working on low-value tasks, etc.)

- Speeding up

- Giving up

Here are some *effective* responses to being overloaded:

- Think – slow down and remember that 80 percent of your results come from 20 percent of your efforts. There is a very good chance that 80 percent of what you think you need to do, *does not matter*. Stop trying to do it all! Contrary to what you want to believe, you are not exempt from the 80/20 rule.

- Clarify – the antidote to confusion is clarity. Stop and ask questions. Ask yourself, ask others. Clarify what you need to do and why you need to do it. Clarify the outcome you truly desire.

- Simplify – Break up overwhelming projects into digestible tasks.

- Eliminate – Think about reasons you should not do something or legitimate ways you can avoid doing it. Is it your priority or someone else's? Should you not accept the task? Should you delegate it? Should you forget it?

- Shut down – If things are totally out of control, take the most counterintuitive action of all. Shut down and make getting organized your highest priority. Forget anything that isn't absolutely life sustaining for a few hours or even a few days, and get under control.

If you find yourself running through life,
at least take the time to ask yourself
where you are going...and why.

38
Interruptions

What?

Frequently stopping and restarting when working on a project or task is a significant productivity killer. Here's a simple time management tip...*stop stopping so much and you will get more done in less time.*

So What?

Some people have become so reactive-responsive that they believe they can't sit still and concentrate anymore. However, anyone who can sit through a movie has the ability to stick to the task at hand. Think about it, if you can stick with a movie, you have proven you are capable of sustained concentration for a couple of hours. Of course, it helps that movie theaters usually do a great job of minimizing distractions when the main feature starts. Conditions are right for concentrating on one thing...the movie. Try the same thing at work. Minimize any distractions and focus on the main event. When you sit down and start working on a project, don't stop until you finish it. And remember, an overwhelming project is always made up of a lot of little projects. Pick one of the little projects and finish it from beginning to end. Then, use the time you've saved by not stopping and starting to go enjoy a good movie.

Now What?

Set appointments with yourself and stick to them. Let's say you need a couple of hours to concentrate on a particular project tomorrow. You decide to work on the project from 10 a.m. until noon, but you do not put it on your calendar. Meanwhile, someone calls and asks if you can meet with them at 10:30 the next morning. You glance at your calendar and see nothing scheduled and say, "Sure, why not." They have, in effect, stolen your time. Of course, you don't want to say, "I've got an appointment with myself." You simply tell them, "I've already got something scheduled for that time tomorrow. Can we do it another time?" The majority of the time, the other person will accommodate you and look for another time to meet with you. And you remain in control of one of your most valuable resources...your time.

Stop interrupting yourself. Stop letting other people interrupt you so much. Learn to concentrate and stick with a project. Interruptions are going to occur. It's a way of life these days. Just try to minimize them.

Look for ways you interrupt yourself or ways you let others interrupt you. You can't stop all of them, but you can stop most of them.

39
Clarify and Begin

What?

Here's an example that illustrates the power of clarity:

- *Scenario 1* – Someone goes to the grocery store to get something for you without knowing what you want. Since there are 60,000 to 100,000 different items in many large grocery stores, it is going to be a difficult "project" for them to handle.

- *Scenario 2* – You ask the person to get you some milk. The project, in this case, will be much easier, but you can still have problems. They might bring you a pint of chocolate milk when what you need is a gallon of skim milk.

- *Scenario 3* – You ask the person to get you one gallon of a certain brand of skim milk. Suddenly, the project is very easy to handle.

The only difference in scenario one and scenario three is clarification. It made a huge difference in this case, and it will make a huge difference in getting anything done.

So What?

Do not start something or ask others to start on something until you have taken the time to clarify the results or outcome you expect and desire. Learn to balance your actions by establishing a long-term vision and a short-term focus. Focusing too much or too little on either of these extremes can negatively impact your productivity.

Now What?

Think about what you are trying to accomplish. Clarify your intentions as much as possible without overthinking what you want to do. Get started and make necessary adjustments as you go.

Think of the most important thing you want to do in your life right now. Spend a reasonable amount of time clarifying your intentions. This is the first step. By doing this, you have officially started. If something is important to you, *when* you are going to start doing it is more important than *how* you are going to get it done. Think about it today and begin taking action today.

There is only one good answer to the question of when you should begin something that is important to you...that answer is, Right Now!

40
Getting Started

What?

There is a time when chaos comes in handy. How many times have you struggled to get started on something and when you finally got started, everything was easy from then on? Consider getting off to a chaotic start. You can go back to your more methodical and sane ways after you have the project rolling forward.

So What?

Many people procrastinate or fail to start something because they try to "get it right" on the front end. It's much easier to get started on something, and revise it or improve it, than to get it right the first time.

Now What?

Here's a good way to get things going when you are stuck.

Get a few people (preferably some out-of-the-box thinkers) in a room with a stack of index cards. Write the topic you want to explore or the project you want to start on a flipchart or grease board. Pause and give everybody a minute or two to think about the topic and ask them to write each idea they have on a separate index card. Then debrief the group by asking them to read their ideas out loud and toss their index card in the middle of the table. As one person reads their idea out loud, instruct the others to try to come up with other ideas that are triggered by the reader's idea. Keep doing this until you have a lot of ideas on cards in the middle of the table.

Then categorize the ideas and group cards with similar or related ideas together. Ask the group to point to the best idea and turn the index card explaining the idea facedown. Then determine the next best idea and turn the card explaining that idea facedown on top of the first one. Keep doing this until all the cards are facedown. Then turn the stack of cards over. You now have plenty of ideas to help you get started, and they are organized in priority order. Assign the cards to people who will follow up on the ideas and get started on your project. The meeting will seem a little chaotic at first, but you will end up with a highly organized plan of action.

Other Applications

Use this technique in the following situations:

- Making hiring decisions
- Solving problems
- Preparing speeches or presentations
- Preparing proposals
- Designing products
- Designing processes

**The first steps and the last steps
are usually the hardest.**

41
The Parable of the Spindle

What?

In college, we evaluated a case study called *The Parable of the Spindle*. One of the main points of the case was that in many restaurants, cooks and chefs were considered higher status employees than waiters. Whether this was right or wrong is not the point. The point is that waiters were "giving orders" to the cooks and this caused considerable tension. Someone came up with the idea of using a spindle, like you still see in many restaurant kitchens.

The spindle solves several problems. The waiters no longer give the cooks verbal orders. The written orders are attached to the spindle and submitted in a much more organized fashion. It is easier for the cooks to decide what to do next; the spindle rotates and the orders come up in priority order. Everybody feels more comfortable and the new process helps get things done in a more organized and appropriate fashion.

So What?

If this simple process works for cooks and waiters…it will work for you and your projects.

Now What?

All the popular word processing software programs have a "table" function. You can easily create tables to serve as your "electronic spindle" for projects you work on or manage. Although sophisticated project management software is available, a word processing table document is a simple solution that's easy to learn. Simply create a table with the following columns:

- Category of the item (for example, People, Products, Processes, Resources or any categories that make sense for your particular project)
- What is to be done
- Who will do it
- When they will do it
- A column for general comments, if needed
- A column to keep up with the status of the item (in-process, completed, etc.)

Then, *sort the table by date* and you are ready to get started on your project. This is also a great way to monitor the progress of projects you manage. You simply glance at the table each day and see what is scheduled for completion and what is still pending. You can revise the document and re-sort it if unexpected items need to be added to the project plan. It's a great way to stay on top of anything that is important to you.

There are three potential problems with planning...no planning, not enough planning and overplanning. Keep it as simple as possible.

42
Speed-reading

What?

Speed-reading is a skill they should have taught you in school, but they didn't.

So What?

Are you looking for a ridiculously easy way to find the time to get more done? Here's a way you can easily gain over three weeks of productive time each year by simply using one finger.

When you were a child, you probably ran one finger along the lines of the book as you read a story. At some point in time, a grown-up told you this was not a good idea and encouraged you to learn to read without using your finger…like "big people" do. As it turns out, the "big people" were wrong. Using your finger as a guide and keeping your eyes slightly ahead of your finger as you read, can easily double your reading speed. Assuming you have at least an hour's worth of reading material to tackle every working day, you will save 30 minutes a day by using this finger-reading method. A typical work year for most people is 260 days. Therefore, you save 130 hours a year by reading twice as fast. That's over three weeks a year! Using this method paces your reading better and keeps you from backtracking so much. Try it right now...it works!

Most people think reading faster reduces their ability to concentrate and retain the information they are reading. As it turns out, this is also wrong. You actually improve your ability to comprehend and retain information when you read faster. This is just one example of how speed-reading can help you get more done with less effort.

Now What?

You can learn to speed-read by attending a course, taking a self-study course or reading a book on speed-reading. Here are two of my personal favorites:

- *10 Days to Faster Reading* by Abby Marks-Beale

- *Quantum Reading* by Bobbi DePorter with Mike Hernacki

If you combine the two books mentioned above, they contain about 150 pages, including many blank pages and pictures. Even a slow reader could probably read them in two to four hours. In addition to the finger-reading technique, there are enough ideas in these books to help you easily double or quadruple your reading speed in a very short time.

Would you be willing to invest two to four hours in something tomorrow that could help you gain six or more weeks of productive time each year? It's a better idea than complaining you don't have the time to get it all done. Try it!

43

Overcome Your Tendency to Get Overwhelmed

What?

Learn to stop…when you think you should go! It is very counterintuitive for most people to do this. However, when you learn to do this, your productivity (and life) will improve.

So What?

People often like to brag about how busy they are and how much they have going on. However, if you consistently feel overwhelmed, here's what is really going on:

- You are setting unrealistic time frames for what you are trying to do.

- You are procrastinating too long.

- You are spending too much time working on things that do not matter.

- You are over-promising what you can do for someone.

- You do not have the profound knowledge needed to do the task.

- You do not know when and how to say "No."

The list can go on and on, but here's the point. All of these reasons have two things in common. Feeling overwhelmed is the result of faulty thinking and making some bad choices in the past. The solution is stunningly simple. Change your thinking and begin making better choices right now...today...this minute. Quit making choices that lead you down the path to being stressed-out, anxious and overwhelmed. The typical response to anxiety is action. Action drives out thought. Doing something without thinking about it creates anxiety...and the cycle continues.

Now What?

The job of a problem is to get your attention. Being overwhelmed is a problem. Therefore, being frequently overwhelmed should be a sign that you are doing something wrong. Look around. There are people doing what you do without being overwhelmed. There are people doing much more than you are doing without being overwhelmed. The workload isn't the real problem...it's how you approach your work that is the problem. For example, take the speed-reading tip in Chapter 42:

- *The problem* – I can't get everything read that I need to read.

- *Overwhelmed person's response* – I've got to work harder and more hours and get all this stuff read.

- *A much better response* – I've got to stop chasing after this problem right now and learn to speed-read. It may feel counterintuitive right now, but it's a great long-term solution to this problem.

> **When you encounter a problem, stop and ask yourself, "What's the real problem? How can I make it go away?"**

44
Procrastination

What?

I kept putting off writing this chapter for some reason. Just kidding! Technically, to procrastinate means to postpone doing something. Sometimes it's a good idea to postpone certain things. Usually it's a good idea to postpone making a snap judgment about something or someone. Sometimes you postpone "important things" you need to do, and they miraculously disappear or no longer matter. Procrastination only becomes dysfunctional behavior when it begins to negatively impact your life...when it keeps you from living the life you desire.

So What?

Procrastination has many potential sources. Here are a few of the more common ones:

- Perfectionism – the paralyzing need to get it right the first time
- Impulsiveness – taking on too many things to do and overloading yourself
- Fear of failure – rather be seen as lacking in effort than ability
- Perception of task – seems too hard or too boring
- Uncertainty – not sure what to do

Now What?

Realize you are never going to totally stop procrastinating. Look for the three or four areas of procrastination that are hurting you the most. For example:

- If you are in sales and you avoid prospecting.
- If you are a writer and you don't write.
- If you are a manager and you don't delegate.
- If you are a parent and you don't spend time with your children.
- If you have dreams and you don't act on your dreams.

When you find yourself procrastinating, first see if you can eliminate the task. Decide what will happen if you just don't do it. For the things you can't eliminate, conquer them one at a time. Pick the area of procrastination that is bothering you the most and set a weekly or daily appointment with yourself to focus on it. By focus, I mean allow no distractions unless things like bleeding, respiratory failure and other events that call for a 911 response are involved. Build on your success and go on to the next area of procrastination that is bothering you and tackle it. Keep tackling the issues until you've got all the big ones under control.

**Stop procrastinating on how to
deal with procrastination.**

45
Perfectionism

What?

Perfectionism is yet another form of dysfunctional behavior disguised as a positive personality attribute. Before the majority of the perfectionists reading this tune me out, let me clarify my position on this:

- The pursuit of excellence and mastery is a noble activity...I like it!

- Perfectionism is an irrational, illogical and potentially neurotic activity...I don't like it!

Being a perfectionist and being organized are not very compatible.

So What?

Perfectionism drains the productivity and energy of the perfectionist. It can literally paralyze people and keep them from starting on important projects and tasks. It is hard to get organized and be more productive if you are paralyzed.

One of the primary sources of perfectionism is criticism. It could be that you grew up in an environment where your parents, teachers, peers or other people important to you were, shall we say, slightly overcritical. But don't be too quick to lay the blame on others. It could be that a part of your psyche took on the role of mental parent and criticized yourself. You decided to develop your own little internal voice to provide all the criticism you needed. You may have decided to play the children's version of "keeping up with the Joneses." You picked a big brother or sister, or a high-achieving peer, and decided to be like them...or be better than them. You began living your life by comparison. If you didn't always measure up, your little voice was quick to let you know about it. Think about it. People who are frequently criticized pay a high price for mistakes. Therefore, they respond by vowing to get it right the first time or not doing anything unless they do it exceptionally well.

Now What?

First of all...chill out! Lighten up! Go ahead and take a chance every once in a while. Make a few mistakes. Won't it feel good not to always take on the role of propping up the business, family, relationship, project or world? Then look for the birth of your critical voice. Where did it begin? Was it someone else? Was it you? Turn that voice off! As with most forms of dysfunctional behavior, discover the source and you have much of the problem solved. And if you decide to find out the source of your perfectionist behavior, don't look for the perfect answer. Look for an excellent answer and live with it.

There is a huge difference in perfectionism and the pursuit of excellence or mastery. Perfectionists never feel satisfied. They always feel somewhat restless and disappointed in their performance. In short, their activities generate more negative feelings than positive feelings. Although masters also know they can improve their skills or performance, they feel a sense of satisfaction and accomplishment when they perform their work. In short, their activities generate positive feelings and enhance self-esteem. Pursue excellence or mastery and stop being a perfectionist.

Remember, a true friend is someone who really knows you and still likes you. Learn to be your own best friend.

46
Profound Knowledge

What?

How do some people get so much *more* done in so much *less* time than others? They have a *profound knowledge* of what they are doing.

So What?

Take any job and think about how much better and quicker you could do it if you totally understood what needs to be done and how to do it. In spite of this obvious fact, many people go right on trying to do their job with a superficial knowledge of how to do it. This idea applies to every person and every job that exists on this planet. Here's an example of how this works:

> Seasoned transplant surgeons can perform incredibly complex surgical operations with ease...but it may take them hours to fix a running toilet when they get home after a day of performing miracles and saving lives.
>
> Seasoned plumbers may be able to easily fix a running toilet in a few minutes...but would you want to have them perform your transplant surgery?

In their own way, these people have ended up in the same place in life. They know how to do their respective jobs well because they took the time to develop a profound knowledge of what needs to be done and how to do it. But try to switch jobs on them and you will quickly see the effects of a lack of profound knowledge. When you switch the jobs, it will take *more* time to get *less* done...if the job gets done at all.

Now What?

There's an old saying, "What's in the well, comes up in the bucket." Here are some great ways to fill up your "knowledge well" so you will have what you need when your "bucket" comes up.

Read – Learn in a few hours or minutes what it took the author years to learn. One common trait among most high achievers is their commitment to reading and ongoing improvement. Be sure and try any good ideas you read about. Remember, you can't lose weight by reading a diet book. You've got to try the diet.

Hang around masters – Find out who is among the best at your job and hang around them and learn from them. Especially hang around masters who have specific knowledge related to your calling in life.

Make sure you are passionate about your job – Everything else falls into place more easily if you love what you are doing. Discover your true calling in life and get on a path to mastering the knowledge related to your passion.

Stop making excuses and start learning more about your job than anyone else within a 100-mile radius of your workspace. When you accomplish this, move your radius out another 100 miles. Keep this up until you don't have anymore room to expand your radius.

47
Irrational Thoughts and To-Do Lists

What?

When an irrational thought passes through your mind, it does not necessarily mean you are crazy. You may or may not be crazy, but all of us frequently have irrational thoughts. There is one fairly common irrational thought that drains our energy and keeps many of us from doing our best in life.

**I have to do all the things that I want to do...
or that someone else wants me to do.**

So What?

It's hard to get rid of a thought like this, but if you can learn to tone it down a bit, you will free up a significant amount of energy to devote to some of your more rational thoughts. This thought is especially counterproductive for people who love to create to-do lists.

One of the problems with using a to-do list is that most people make it *too easy for things to get on the list*. They constantly develop extensive to-do lists, but never seem to find the time to do most things on the lists. Many people love to cross things off their to-do list so much, that when they complete a task that was not on their list, they actually take the time to write it down just so they can cross it off. Putting something on your to-do list usually initiates the unfinished-business-cycle-of-guilt. Because it is now in writing, you feel like you have to do it. Every time you look at the unfinished item, you experience a little drain in your energy level.

Now What?

Here's an idea for you to-do list junkies...*spend as much time figuring out how to prevent things from getting on your to-do list in the first place, as you do filling up your to-do list with low priority, meaningless items.* I know what many of you are thinking. That's not my problem! Everything on my to-do list is very important. Surveys, studies and statistics prove that most of you are wrong. If you must use a to-do list to monitor and control your priorities, filter the busywork and low-value tasks out of your list daily.

Follow-up forms and hanging files discussed in previous chapters of this book provide an alternative to to-do lists that work more effectively for many people. You can keep up with each task individually. You don't have to rewrite your list when it gets too long or out-of-date. You can use the follow-up forms and the 1 to 31 and January to December files to effectively and efficiently keep up with your workflow. Follow-up items are filed away based on when you plan to do them, off your mind for now, and not constantly draining your energy as an unmarked item on your to-do list. And as you can see in the chapter on prioritizing, you can usually prioritize your work in 60 seconds or less using the 1 to 31 hanging file system.

Here's one more tip for people who like to try to do it all. Set up a hanging file labeled "Someday/Maybe." Put all the items you want to do, but do not have to do, in this file. If you find your-self with a lot of free time on your hands after you have complet-ed the things you have to do…reach in the Someday/Maybe file and go for it! If you have totally run out of high priority items…these are great things to work on. In my case, I constant-ly put things in my Someday/Maybe file during the month. It at least gets them off my mind and I don't feel guilty about not working on them. At the end of the month, I usually dump the contents of the file in the trash.

A person is never what he ought to be until he is doing what he ought to be doing.

48
Saying No!

What?

Learn to say no when it is appropriate.

So What?

Are you still having trouble getting everything done after all these ideas I have shared with you? If so, are you one of those people who *talks about* the value of saying "no," or do you actually say "no" to people and activities that do not fit into your priorities?

Now What?

If you are not good at saying no, here is a technique that may be helpful to you:

Place the tip of your tongue on the roof of your mouth – slightly behind your front teeth – and grin. As you release your tongue, utter the sound "nuuuuuh" and resolve this process by forming a sort of "fish-mouth" circle with your lips and entire mouth...and clearly articulate the sound "oooooo!" Practice this technique 10 minutes a day for the next three days. The next time someone tries to distract you from your priorities, show them the new technique for dealing with distractions that you have learned.

"No" is not a four-letter word!

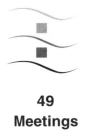

49
Meetings

What?

The good...the bad...and the ugly! That pretty much sums things up on the topic of meetings. There are good ones, bad ones and ugly ones.

So What?

Stop going to bad or ugly meetings. Stop conducting bad or ugly meetings. Meetings are often necessary, so if you must have one, make it a productive use of everyone's time.

Now What?

Here are a few quick tips to help get your meetings going in the right direction.

- Clarify and clearly communicate the purpose of your meeting. The more you clarify, the more you increase your chances of having a successful meeting.

- After you clarify your purpose, try to find any legitimate reason to avoid having the meeting. Can things be handled in a memo or an e-mail? Would one-on-one conversations be as or more effective?

- Are the right people invited to your meeting? Are people included that don't need to be there?

- Can materials be sent to attendees prior to the meeting to facilitate discussions or decisions?

- Be ruthless about starting and ending on time.

- Do not allow off-topic discussions. Use a flipchart or pad of paper to capture these items and handle them later. Get back on the topic of the meeting as soon as you capture these off-topic ideas.

- Have one person designated as a recorder to take notes for everyone and distribute the notes to all meeting attendees. Everyone except the recorder needs to listen and stay mentally engaged in the meeting.

- Establish a clear plan for what happens next for any follow-up items. Who will do it? What will they do? When will they do it?

To learn more about conducting effective meetings read *Death by Meeting* by Patrick M. Lencioni and *How to Make Meetings Work* by Michael Doyle and David Straus.

Meetings are prime candidates for the list of massive time-wasting activities. Don't look for ways to justify them, look for ways to justify not having them. If you genuinely can't figure out a way to avoid a meeting...have a good one.

50
Personality Mismatches

What?

Would you give a 100-pound person a 300-pound job?

Imagine a 100-pound person trying to be a lineman for a professional football team. Now imagine a 300-pound person trying to be a jockey. You can easily observe the physical characteristics of these two and determine you have a mismatch on your hands. But what if you switched the two? By doing this, you significantly increase their chances of success in their respective roles.

So What?

Personality characteristics work in the same way…it's just harder to observe them. However, personality mismatching negatively impacts productivity and performance just like physical mismatching. For example:

- Giving a highly spontaneous, fast-paced person a job that requires a methodical, steady approach.

- Giving an introvert a job that calls for extrovert behavior.

- Giving an abstract thinker a job that calls for concrete thinking.

- Giving a person who favors logic over emotions a job that calls for a high level of tolerance and sympathy.

This mismatching goes on every day in every business because employers and managers fail to understand the power of matching a person's job responsibilities with their personality characteristics.

Now What?

It is estimated that the cost of a bad hire can easily exceed the annual compensation of a mismatched employee. But it's not just money at stake here. It's poor morale, excessive waste of time and resources, loss of customers and many other negative issues brought on by mismatching. Of course, in the end, all of these issues translate into loss of money for your business.

Take a few moments to find out how personality profiling can help you improve the bottom line of your business. It usually takes a very small amount of time and money to prevent the majority of mismatches that occur in most businesses. There are many excellent tools available to help match people's jobs with their personalities. Take advantage of them and end this resource-draining problem as soon a possible. And don't forget to consider the most important match of all...your own job and your own personality.

Stop putting 100-pound people in 300-pound jobs. It's costing you too much money and frustration, and it can be easily prevented.

51
Psychological Dysfunctions

What?

Due to their special circumstances, some people struggle with ideas that make perfect sense to others. If you suffer from Chronic Disorganization (CD) or Attention Deficit Disorder (ADD), you can learn some special techniques to help you cope with the resulting problems. If you manage a person who suffers from these dysfunctions, you need to be aware of how you can help them with their disorganization problems.

So What?

For most people, "out of sight, out of mind" is a casual part of their belief system. They genuinely believe they will struggle or lose track of things if they can't physically see them on top of their desk. After learning some sound organizing techniques, they often change their minds and feel comfortable putting things away in an orderly manner. However, some individuals with CD or ADD *really do need to keep things in sight*. Putting things away in a file cabinet would make them so uncomfortable that it would be totally counterproductive. These people may need to organize things in a totally different way. They may need to store things in clear, see-through containers or create an entirely different file labeling system to help them cope with their difficulties.

Many people struggle with disorganization because they have other issues they must deal with before any organizing system will help. These problems run the gamut from simple forms of self-defeating behavior to significant psychological dysfunctions. Most of us are not qualified – and should not try – to handle serious psychological disorders. The goal here is simply to raise the level of awareness concerning these issues and point people in the right direction for help if they need it. Again, even people without these problems need to know the problems exist so they will be realistic in their efforts to lead and manage people with these challenges.

Now What?

Here are some good places to start if you want to know more about these topics. I highly recommend taking a look at Judith Kolberg's book on conquering chronic disorder. If you think it is relevant to you or your employees, try some of the other books as well.

- *Conquering Chronic Disorganization* by Judith Kolberg
- *I'm OK – You're OK* by Thomas A. Harris, M.D.
- *ADD-Friendly Ways to Organize Your Life* by Judith Kolberg & Kathleen Nadeau, Ph.D.
- *Get Out of Your Own Way* by Mark Goulston, M.D. and Philip Goldberg
- *An Adult Child's Guide to What's "Normal"* by John Friel, Ph.D. & Linda Friel, M.A.
- *Recovery: A Guide for Adult Children of Alcoholics* by Herbert L. Gravitz and Julie D. Bowden

We are not all the same. Our strengths and struggles are quite different and often quite hidden from ourselves and others.

52
Homeostasis Hump

What?

No matter how easy something might be, or how much you want to do something, if it requires you to change your behavior, *there will be a period of time when even the most enthusiastic adapters among you will encounter some mysterious, internally generated resistance.* I call this the "homeostasis hump." In terms of getting organized, homeostasis means…people do not like change. Homeostasis is all about staying in your comfort zone, even when staying there is bad for you.

So What?

Homeostasis can *hurt* you by putting up resistance to the changes you want to make, or it can *help* you with the changes. Here's an example of how it works. In the old days, people were not required to wear seat belts. Most cars didn't even have them. In the '60s and '70s, they started enacting seat belt laws. Suddenly, people *had to* wear seat belts…they were mandated by law. Some people panicked. The doomsday-types were just getting over their fear of running their car with those newfangled power windows in a pond and flipping upside down. As they were thinking about the possibility of getting trapped in the bottom of the pond with malfunctioning windows, another killer device disguised as a lifesaving innovation was forced upon them…seat belts. Now they would be doubly trapped, strapped in, windows closed, drowned and dead! Other people intellectually agreed with the concept and still had a hard time remembering to fasten their new seat belts. At first, homeostasis fought everybody.

But here we are many years later. I don't know about you, but when I get in my car…or when my children get in my car…we do not go anywhere until everybody fastens their seat belts. There are now times when I get a block away from my home and realize *something is wrong…something doesn't feel right*. I look down and realize I haven't fastened my seat belt. I am, in effect, over the homeostasis hump. Now, wearing my seat belt is my normal state. Any change in this normal state will be met with internal resistance. Homeostasis is now helping me instead of fighting me.

Now What?

If you want to get over the homeostasis hump with anything in your life, one way to increase your chances of success is to pick an accountability partner. Pick another person interested in making the same change and identify the specific habit or habits you want to change. Then work on making the change together. You will significantly increase the odds of forming new organizing habits if you work with someone else. Go choose a partner right now. Tell them what you are up to and ask them if they want to join you.

**Homeostasis can help you or
hurt you…it's your choice.**

53
Three Possible Outcomes

What?

Anytime you encounter a new idea, there are three possible outcomes.

1. Nothing will happen.
2. You will alter your behavior in some minor ways.
3. The idea will significantly change your behavior and your life forever.

So What?

Did you ever wonder why different people experience such different outcomes from the same experience? Consider this. Assume three people encounter a 5-foot snake in the woods. Now assume one person, a city dweller, had a bad experience with a snake as a child. Another person grew up on a farm and frequently encountered snakes around the barn. And the third person was Steve Irwin (better known as TV's *The Crocodile Hunter*). The city dweller will probably run in fear or look for a weapon. The farm-raised person will nonchalantly move on, respecting the snake's right to exist in peace. And then there's the Crocodile Hunter. Steve will probably get excited, run over and pick up the snake, play with it, chat with it for a few minutes, have a lot of fun with it and then set it free. In this example, the same event – being surprised by a snake – resulted in three different responses. The *different outcomes* were the result of three *different belief systems* about snakes.

This example illustrates that knowledge and understanding can help eliminate fears. It also shows the influence of belief systems on outcomes. Good ideas can help you alter your belief systems. But it is up to you to *connect the idea to the belief system that needs altering*.

Now What?

When you are dissatisfied with an outcome in your life and you want to change it…you must examine and disrupt the belief system that is driving that outcome. The belief system must be changed if you want the outcome to change. Most of the pathways in our brains are formed early in life. Evaluate this time in your life if you want to determine some of your most powerful belief systems. For example, salespeople having trouble selling often remember the feelings associated with these instructions from their childhood:

- "Don't talk to strangers."
- "Children are to be seen and not heard."
- "Don't stick your nose in other people's business."

These old messages are still in the inner recesses of their brain making them feel bad about meeting new clients, prospecting and asking qualifying questions.

Some of the beliefs that were installed in your brain when you were young are still serving you well. Some are not. Therein lies the key. Constantly challenge the details of your belief system.

Have fun discovering and eliminating the beliefs that limit your potential. Examine your long-held beliefs related to money, your career, your family and your personal relationships. And most importantly, examine your long-held beliefs about yourself. If a particular belief is still serving you well, keep it around. If not, change the belief to something that will support the outcome you desire. The key to changing your behavior is changing your beliefs.

Take the time to understand your own behavior. Learn why you do the things you do. You will undoubtedly discover some huge surprises.

54
Now What?

What?

You've almost finished the book.

So What?

Reading about getting organized will not make you an organized person.

Now What?

Read the last chapter and try some of the ideas in this book...right now! But remember, homeostasis will fight against even minor behavior changes, so don't try too many of the ideas at one time. Homeostasis really doesn't like multiple changes at once.

55
Peace of Mind Productivity

What?

Let's wrap this book up with a few thoughts on success and peace of mind. One of the main benefits of living a successful life is that you *occasionally* find yourself in a peaceful state of mind. When peacefulness sporadically appears in your life, it relays a message to your body and soul to relax and enjoy the moment. Learn to savor peace of mind when it appears and it will appear more often. Peacefulness prefers to be noticed. It likes to know it is welcome in your life. Your attention and appreciation encourage it to return more often.

Success means different things to different people. However you personally define success, make sure it includes occasional interludes of peacefulness, calmness, serenity and satisfaction.

So What?

What does all this have to do with getting more focused, organized and productive? *A peaceful state of mind is the ultimate reason for getting more focused, organized and productive.* Productivity ideas are not all the same. You can learn slash-and-burn techniques that will help you wring a little more productivity out of your life and out of other people. These ideas are usually all about working harder, working faster and getting the most out of people. *Good* productivity ideas are about feeling engaged, working at a satisfying pace and getting the best out of people.

Now What?

It's all about balance. This book is not written for people who are seeking nirvana or utopia. This book is for practical people who think practically and realistically, and want to be successful in the real world.

Writing books is one of my passions. I hope many of the ideas in this book help you realize your passions. Remember, the ideas offered in this book are only suggestions. They may not all be right for you, but they are the best ideas I have to share with you on this topic at this point in my life.

Winston Churchill once said:

"Writing a book is an adventure. To begin with, it is a toy and an amusement; then it becomes a mistress, and then it becomes a master, and then a tyrant. The last phase is that just as you are about to be reconciled to your servitude, you kill the monster, and fling him out to the public."

This not only applies to writing books. It applies to all of you who are waiting until you "absolutely get it right" before you share your passions with the world. I wish you much success and peace of mind. Get focused, organized and productive. Find your true calling in life, and fling your ideas and talents out into the world!

Additional Reading and Thinking

I hope you enjoyed *Getting Organized*. My goal was to keep the book as short as possible, so busy people could find the time to read it. Most chapters were highly distilled versions of books I have read, ideas I have developed, or techniques I have learned from others. For those of you who want to learn more about some of the ideas presented, this section includes some additional resources or things to think about for most of the chapters in this book. Several books will come up many times in these notes on additional reading and thinking. The more times a book is mentioned, the more benefit you will get from reading it.

There are no additional resources provided on the chapters related to setting up the various hanging files. Just give them a try! Of course, many of you may be satisfied with your current physical filing system and only want to try some of the mental techniques to help you get more organized. Whatever you decide, I wish you much success in your efforts to become more organized and productive. Thanks for choosing to spend some time reading my book.

1. Why Can't I Get Organized?

Think about it...looking for the "one right answer" is rarely the best way to approach problem solving. Especially when there may be at least six different issues causing your problem.

Remember that disorganization is a symptom of a problem, not the problem. If you want to increase the chances that you will find lasting solutions to your productivity problems, look for multiple solutions. Don't give up on getting organized just because you have tried something – or several things – that didn't work. Roger von Oech's books, *A Whack on the Side of the Head* and *A Kick in the Seat of the Pants* are excellent resources to learn more about how to look for more than one right answer.

2. Simplicity

Think about it…in *The 80/20 Principle*, the author Richard Koch states: "The act of making a business complex depresses returns more effectively than any other means known to humanity." The same is true of your life. Complexity reduces productivity and joy more effectively than any other means. Keep it simple…it works!

3. Physical Activity Always Follows Mental Activity

Book: *As a Man Thinketh* by James Allen – This is the granddaddy of all self-help books. This book gets to the bottom of things good and bad in your life. It is a fact; whatever you think about expands in your life. James Allen teaches you how to think your way to a better life. Read it slowly and reflect on every sentence, on every page…and begin to choose your thoughts more carefully. This book can literally change your life overnight!

4. Get Your Habits Right and Defeat the Beast

Book: *Help Yourself to Happiness* by Maxie C. Maultsby, Jr., M.D. – Dr. Maultsby shows you how and which of your habits generate much of your self-defeating behavior, and how you can get rid of these habits fast. The book helps you learn how to convert irrational thinking to rational thinking. Remaining alive or surviving is not enough. Use the ideas in this book to remain happily alive...with a maximum of joy, pleasure, satisfaction and self-fulfillment.

5. The Monkey Trap

Book: *Get Out of Your Own Way* by Mark Goulston, M.D., and Philip Goldberg – It's bad enough when other people become obstacles to your success, but it's worse when you are the culprit. Many people seem to carry a loaded weapon around pointed at their own feet. Whenever success begins to creep into their lives, they fire the weapon. These authors discuss 40 traps (they refer to them as examples of self-defeating behavior) to watch out for and offer excellent suggestions on how to avoid them. These traps are the adult version of "running with scissors." Your mother should have let you run with scissors and told you not to do these things instead. The scissors wouldn't have done near as much damage to your life as these counterproductive, and unfortunately, very common behaviors. Read this book and put your loaded gun away.

6. A Few Thoughts on Gadget-based Solutions

Think about it...why do we have so many new timesaving devices, but gain so little additional time by using these gadgets? Some of them will work for you and some of them won't. Some of the gadgets that work for others will not work for you and vice versa. Use the gadgets that make sense and actually help you...but do not believe all the promises you hear in the advertisements. And do not keep using something that is not working for you just because you spent money on it.

7. Right Now...!

Book: *Slowing Down to the Speed of Life* by Richard Carlson and Joseph Bailey – This book points out the fact that the world is not going to accommodate you by making fewer demands on your time and energy. You must learn how to dismiss the distractions from your mind and focus on one thing at a time. The authors suggest many excellent ways you can learn to do this. This book is for people who feel like they are always rushing, but never catching up.

8. "To Do or Not to Do?"...That is the Question

Book: *The 80/20 Principle* by Richard Koch – This book offers many solutions to productivity problems. Use it to help you determine what to keep doing and what to quit doing. Look up John Gagliardi on the Internet and learn more about how he consistently creates successful teams.

9. The 80/20 Rule

Books: *The 80/20 Principle* and *The 80/20 Individual* by Richard Koch – For millions of years, nobody realized the true value of sand. It was lying all around mankind in abundance, but nobody paid too much attention to it. Then someone learned how to convert the silicon in sand into microprocessors and memory chips. Think about what has become of that little discovery. An Italian economist, Vilfredo Pareto, came up with an incredibly powerful idea in the late 1800s called the "Pareto Principle" or the "80/20 Rule." Simply stated, he, and others who later expanded on his findings, discovered that 80 percent of our results come from 20 percent of our efforts. Most people allow this idea to lie around like sand. They don't use it to create amazing things in their lives. A few people have understood the power of this idea...they have become the human equivalent of supercomputers. These two books can teach you how to use this powerful idea.

10. The Best Reason to Get Organized

Think about it...feelings are the only direct source of knowledge we have. Everything else we know or have learned is second-hand knowledge. Two things ultimately motivate people: seeking positive feelings and avoiding negative feelings. Learn to track your feelings to their source. Find out what is causing your positive and negative feelings. If it's legal and appropriate, the fact that something makes you feel good is a great reason to keep doing it.

11. Having a Definite Purpose

Book: *Think and Grow Rich* by Napoleon Hill – Knowing your purpose in life is one of the grandest of all problem solvers. Think about how many of your frustrations would disappear if you felt a reasonable sense of certainty about your life purpose (keep in mind it can change as you journey through the passages of life). One of the best sources to help you discover your purpose and develop a plan to achieve it is the book *Think and Grow Rich*. I personally do not usually like self-help books that seem to be based on clichés and promises of getting rich. Therefore, I avoided this book for many years. I should have known a book that has been around for almost 70 years, and is still widely read, has something good to offer. This is a great book. This book helps you convert confusion into focus. Reading this book is a very good use of your time. For those of you who like to think out-of-the-box a little more, *The Purpose of Your Life* by Carol Adrienne is also a good read on this topic.

12. Workaholic Behavior

Book: *Life and Death in the Executive Fast Lane* by Manfred F. R. Kets de Vries – Chapter 14 of this book is titled, "Do Workaholics Have More Fun?" They do if you consider having twice the rate of coronary disease, being five times more likely to have a second coronary attack, and having twice the rate of fatal heart attacks fun. Read this book if you are a workaholic...unless you'd rather not know the outcome of your behavior.

13. Multitasking

Article: *Multitasking Makes You Stupid* by Sue Shellenbarger – This article appeared in the *Wall Street Journal* in late February 2003 and was posted to their online archives on March 1, 2003. You can also find it in several places by conducting a general search on the Internet (search by title or author's name). After reading this article, you may decide that a pattern of multitasking is not such a good idea unless you want to become less efficient, or as the author puts it, "stupider."

14. Clutter is Contagious

Book: *The Tipping Point* by Malcolm Gladwell – In this national best-seller, the author writes about how viruses spread and eventually turn into epidemics. The lessons offered in this book provide powerful clues that show you what happens if you fail to stop the spread of clutter in the beginning. If you fail to stop it in the beginning, you will soon have an epidemic on your hands. It is difficult to live an organized life if you are constantly fighting an epidemic of clutter. There are also many other valuable lessons in this book that can help you create a successful business and/or a successful life.

15. The Proper Order of Events

Article: *Beware the Busy Manager* by Heike and Sumantra Ghoshal from *Harvard Business Review*, February 2002 – This article asks, and then answers, the question, "Are the least effective executives the ones who look like they are doing the most?" You will learn how an astonishing amount of fast-moving activity, allowing little or no time for reflection, is mistakenly thought of as productive behavior by many people. As we mentioned in the chapter on "The Proper Order of Events," sometimes it is best to slow down when you feel like speeding up. This article will offer evidence to support this statement.

16. Gathering Incoming Items

Think about it...the purpose of the chapter on "Gathering Incoming Items" is to help you change your thinking about the incoming items you encounter daily. Thinking of them as individual items that must each be handled uniquely can be overwhelming. Thinking of them as five categories of incoming items that are all processed in the same manner, using the same process, simplifies life and reduces confusion.

36. One Thing at a Time

Book: *Slowing Down to the Speed of Life* by Richard Carlson and Joseph Bailey – This book will help you get your physical and mental lives in harmony. Focus is all about doing something and thinking about what you are doing at the same time. The best way to do this is to do one thing at a time.

37. The Overloaded and Confused Cycle

Book: *The 80/20 Principle* by Richard Koch – Having too many choices can lead to paralysis. This book will help you learn how to sort through your choices and focus on the ones that matter. Keep in mind…most of them don't matter.

38. Interruptions

Think about it…everyone should have some uninterrupted time every day, even if it is just a few minutes a few times a day. If you feel as if you have none, start small and build to a reasonable amount of uninterrupted time as soon as you can. I started with 96 minutes each day. It was so enjoyable and productive; I have now increased it to four hours most days. You may not be able to carve out this much time due to your job responsibilities, but everyone needs some focused time to concentrate on important issues. Stick with your important tasks as long as you can, and you will free up some of the time it takes you to constantly ramp up after excessive interruptions.

39. Clarify and Begin

Book: *Think and Grow Rich* by Napoleon Hill – Here's another good reason to read this book. It's all about developing a clear purpose and a clear plan.

40. Getting Started

Book: *A Whack on the Side of the Head* and *A Kick in the Seat of the Pants* by Roger von Oech – These books will teach you how to get the creative juices flowing. Use the techniques described in these books and you will be able to choose from a plethora of ideas, rather than trying to come up with an idea on how to get started on a project. And these books are fun to read!

41. The Parable of the Spindle

Book: *The Path of Least Resistance* by Robert Fritz – The chapter on "The Parable of the Spindle" is really about developing and documenting a plan. Although this book would not be classified as a strategic or tactical planning book, *The Path of Least Resistance* is the best book I have ever read on the topic of planning. Robert Fritz observes the cycles found in nature and applies them to the planning process. Since Mother Nature rarely gets things wrong, the ideas offered in this book are very sound. The book will help you create the results you desire in your life.

42. Speed-reading

Books: *10 Days to Faster Reading* by Abby Marks-Beale and *Quantum Reading* by Bobbi DePorter with Mike Hernacki – Learning to read faster isn't as hard as you think. Simply set your goal to at least double your speed (a no-brainer using the ideas in these books), and calculate how much time it will save you over the remaining years of your life. The result of your calculation will probably amaze you.

43. Overcome Your Tendency to Get Overwhelmed

Book: *How to Stubbornly Refuse to Make Yourself Miserable About Anything – Yes, Anything!* by Albert Ellis, Ph.D. – Becoming overwhelmed is often the result of irrational thinking. Dr. Ellis will show you how to get rid of many of the irrational thoughts that drive your self-defeating behavior.

44. Procrastination

Article: *Stand and Deliver* by Maia Szalavitz in *Psychology Today*, July/August 2003 – There are plenty of books on the topic of procrastination, but if you want a quick overview of what causes procrastination, read this article. If you want to dig deeper into the topic, try the book *Overcoming Procrastination* by Albert

Ellis, Ph.D., and William J. Knaus, Ed.D. Procrastination is almost always a symptom of a bigger issue. *Overcoming Procrastination* explains the bigger issues and how to deal with them.

45. Perfectionism

Book: *Your Inner Child of the Past* by W. Hugh Missildine, M.D. – This book explains the source of many adult dysfunctions, including perfectionism. Perfectionism often sounds good on the surface, but remember, perfectionism is one of the primary sources of procrastination and other forms of less-than-productive behavior. Understanding the source of unproductive behavior is the first step in effectively dealing with it. Dr. Missildine offers some very interesting thoughts on why people behave in unproductive ways, and how to solve many of the most common adult behavioral problems.

46. Profound Knowledge

Think about it…decide what appropriate reading, thinking or experience makes sense to help you follow up on the chapter on "Profound Knowledge." For example, ask people who are masters in your chosen profession to recommend the best books on your profession. Keep asking until you have a list of books that you feel confident will help you develop a profound knowledge of whatever you have chosen to do with your time, energy and life. Then read and reflect on at least one book a month for the rest of your life. Find a way to work on projects with people who are ahead of you on the path of knowledge related to your profession. Think about what you need to learn to be among the best at what you do for a living. The result of this activity will be more fun and more rewarding.

47. Irrational Thoughts and To-Do Lists

Think about it...if you are going to keep using a to-do list, be extremely discriminating about what you put on this list. And remember; because something is on your to-do list, it does not mean you actually have to do it. Consider eliminating your to-do list and use follow-up forms and the 1 to 31 files to keep up with your priorities.

48. Saying No!

Think about it...several people asked me to elaborate on this idea. I told them "no!"

49. Meetings

Book: *Death by Meeting* by Patrick M. Lencioni – A leadership fable about solving the most painful problem in business: bad meetings. Great book. Fun to read!

50. Personality Mismatches

Book: *Leading Talents, Leading Teams* by Lee Ellis – You only need to read this book if you plan to continue interacting with other human beings. It's as simple as that. If you never plan to hire another person, sell to or persuade another person, lead or manage another person or interact with another person in any way...it's not necessary to read this book. If you think you might find yourself doing any of these things in the future, take the time to learn what Lee Ellis can teach you.

51. Psychological Dysfunctions

Think about it...there are several specific recommendations at the end of the chapter on "Psychological Dysfunctions." The point is you will never get organized if you are struggling with psychological issues that create chaos in your life. You must address these issues first. Clutter, chaos and disorganization are the symptoms, not the causes of your problems. The next time you're in the bookstore, scan a few of the books mentioned in this chapter and see if you recognize yourself in any of the pages.

52. Homeostasis Hump

Think about it…homeostasis has a lot to do with how you are living your life. This internal companion makes many of your daily decisions for you without you being consciously aware of it. Many people think they cannot develop new, highly desired, highly productive habits, when they really are just giving up too soon. Before you begin thinking you can't stick with your plan to change your behavior, learn to stick with new habits until you get over the homeostasis hump.

53. Three Possible Outcomes

Book: *Help Yourself to Happiness* by Maxie C. Maultsby, Jr., M.D. – If you are tired of getting started on self-improvement projects, but never finishing, this is the book for you. Dr. Maultsby offers specific suggestions on how to emotionally re-educate yourself and replace old habits with new ones. He provides some interesting examples of how the feeling part of your brain lags behind the thinking part of your brain. Therefore, you can know how and what you want to do, but feel wrong when you do it. For example, when driving in a foreign country where the custom is to drive on the opposite side of the road, you will intellectually understand which side to drive on, but feel very uncomfortable when doing so. This disconnect between how you think and how you feel is called cognitive dissonance. And cognitive dissonance keeps a lot of us from getting organized.

What's Behind *Getting Organized*?

Getting Organized was written as a result of years of research and training that Chris Crouch has conducted on the topics of improving focus, organization and productivity. His research included the traditional literature on getting organized, but quickly moved to psychology, physiology, anatomy, sociology, philosophy, neurology, mythology, religion, quantum physics and other areas of knowledge typically not thought of as having to do with organizing skills. He found many of the ideas presented in this book in these seemingly unrelated sources.

As a result of his research, Chris also developed the *GO System* training course, a step-by-step process to help people get organized and stay organized. The course has become the "course of choice" for improving productivity by individuals, leaders, managers, professional organizers, coaches, and corporate trainers all over the country. The course includes the following implementation resources:

- a 96-page workbook of ideas and exercises for improving focus, organization and productivity in the workplace

- a step-by-step guide for effectively implementing the ideas presented in the course material

- a bullet-point, quick reference reminder of key course decision

- a laminated, wallet-size reminder card of key ideas to become and stay more organized

- an initial supply of forms for effective implementation and follow-up

- a complete set of file folder tabs for immediate system implementation

- a CD with a variety of implementation resources including forms, labels, and reminders

The research for *Getting Organized* and the *GO System* focused on several questions:

- How can people who get organized, *stay organized*?

- Why don't unorganized people, who say they desperately want to get organized, *do the simple things* that will help them accomplish their goals?

- And the larger but related question...Why don't people *do the things they say they want to do* (and often strongly advise others to do)?

According to Chris, sometimes the answers he found were quite unusual.

"In my study of the human brain and nervous system, I learned about three major systems that have a significant influence on people's behavior. As it turns out these systems, the neocortex, the limbic system and the reticular activating system, have a lot to do with all of the above questions. In its simplest form, the neocortex is the thinking part of the brain, the limbic system is the feeling part of the brain, and the reticular activating system is the "toggle switch" that turns on the neocortex and shuts off the limbic system or vice versa (my apologies to neurosurgeons and neurologists for oversimplifying things). When you are in a state of heightened emotions, the thinking part of your brain shuts off and the feeling part of your brain gets turned on. You re-engage (turn on) the thinking part of your brain by

calming down and relaxing. Here are some implications of this bit of information:

- *Under pressure, you act without thinking (limbic system on/neocortex off).*
- *You can turn the thinking part of your brain back on by relaxing.*
- *If the feeling part of your brain is in control of your behavior, you default to your habits (good or bad).*
- *If you are going to insist on operating under pressure, you must learn good habits.*
- *If you have good habits, it doesn't matter as much which brain system is in control of your behavior.*
- *The feeling part of your brain always lags behind the thinking part of your brain (you can understand something intellectually, but it won't feel right until you keep doing it for a while).*
- *Something that feels right may be bad for you (it's a habit that feels normal).*
- *Something that feels wrong may be good for you (it's not a habit yet).*

There are many other interesting implications and conclusions we could draw just from this one area of knowledge. However, as you can imagine, if I stood in front of a classroom of people who were expecting to hear some ideas on getting organized and started talking about the neocortex, limbic system and reticular activating system...they would probably throw me out of the room."

This example illustrates that there are a lot of solid ideas "under the hood" of *Getting Organized* and the *GO System* to help you conquer your organizing problems once and for all. Try not to discount ideas just because they are presented in simple terms.

The ideas will work if you do one simple thing…try the ideas long enough to get the feeling part of your brain to accept them. The ideas are basically designed to do one of two things:

1. Flip the switch on that activates your thinking brain, or

2. Install good organizing habits in your nervous system for the times you must operate under pressure.

If you look closely at *Getting Organized*, you will see how this knowledge is embedded in the ideas presented.

Getting Organized and the *GO System* are for people who are serious about solving their organizing problems. But you will never lose weight by reading a diet book, you will never learn to paint by reading a book on painting, and you will never get organized by reading a book or attending a training course about getting organized. You must try the ideas until the feeling part of your brain catches up with the thinking part of your brain.

For more information about what's behind *Getting Organized*, to find out about the *GO System* training course or to purchase an implementation kit to help you develop the habits discussed in the book, visit www.thegosystem.com.

About the Author

Chris Crouch is the developer of the *GO System* training course. The course, used all over the country by individuals, leaders, managers, professional organizers, coaches, and corporate trainers, helps improve focus, organization and productivity in the workplace.

Chris has an impressive background in the financial services industry in sales, sales management, and as an executive for a Fortune 500 company. However, his passion has always been reading and learning. Among other topics, he has spent years researching and studying both the mental and physical aspects of getting and staying organized – primarily for his own use. His goal was to find simple, easy-to-implement ideas that work in the real world. Others began requesting that he share this knowledge with them and their employees. Chris regularly writes, speaks and teaches on topics related to productivity. He is president and founder of DME Training and Consulting, and currently lives with his wife and youngest daughter in Memphis, Tenn.

Chris is always looking for ideas to improve productivity. If you have techniques that work for you and are willing to share them with him, or if you would like to discuss any of the ideas presented in this book, please write to Chris at cc@dmetraining.com.